Disciple's Diary

The Meditations and Musings of a Meandering Daughter

CINTHIA W. PRATT

WestBow
PRESS
A DIVISION OF THOMAS NELSON

WestBow Press books may be ordered through booksellers or by contacting:

WestBow Press
A Division of Thomas Nelson
1663 Liberty Drive
Bloomington, IN 47403
www.westbowpress.com
1-(866) 928-1240

ISBN: 978-1-4497-6429-6 (sc)
ISBN: 978-1-4497-6430-2 (e)
ISBN: 978-1-4497-6431-9 (hc)

Library of Congress Control Number: 2012915611

Printed in the United States of America

WestBow Press rev. date: 08/28/2012

Dedication

I offer up praises and thanksgiving to the Lord and Savior, Jesus Christ, who has remained my faithful Shepherd throughout this journey and to the Holy Spirit who authored the words written on these pages. Praise and honor belong to my Father and King who was faithful to accomplish all that He promised.

This humble Disciple's Diary is dedicated to all daughters of the King who are currently on the journey to become everything that He has called them to be. I pray that the Lord might use my words as an instrument to empower, to encourage, and to equip disciple daughters around the globe to boldly go away with their Shepherd when He calls to them. May this book find its way into the hands of each sojourner seeking to know the Lord with all her heart, soul, and mind, and lead her to the freedom that can only be found by securing her identity in Him

And finally, to my husband and spiritual partner, Doug: I love you. Your love and respect have enabled me to walk in obedience to the Lord and afforded me the freedom to move out in ministry and into the whole purpose of what God has for me.

Luke 4:18-19

Table of Contents

Preface

The weather-worn book discovered among the disciple's belongings in the cobweb-covered cardboard box at the back of the attic wasn't much to look at. Its leather cover was cracked and the adhesive at the spine had long given up its fight to hold the diary's yellowed pages in place. The lock and key that had once closely guarded the treasure trove of secret thoughts scribbled inside was broken and most of the contents would now be missing if it were not for the frayed piece of twine that was gingerly wrapped twice and snuggly knotted around the little book.

One quick tug at the string, now feeble with age, sent the storehouse of carefully recorded words tumbling into the air and laid the deeply personal pages bare for all to read. A thicker piece of paper that had been folded into quarters slid down from its once secure hiding place tucked up inside a space within the lining of the diary's outer cover. The book's author must have secretly stashed the paper there long ago. Now as the string gave up its guard the page slipped free and cascaded to the library table below. The curious reader retrieved the paper from the table and delicately smoothed it with her hands until it spread completely out to reveal a hand-sketched map. The faded lines carefully drawn across the ancient map seemed to detail a traveler's journey through what appeared to be a territory from another time and place. The pencil tracings on the map crossed a topography composed of dry desert sands that opened up at one end to a wide expanse of wilderness. The lines on the map also indicated formidable mountain ranges that the diary's owner would have scaled. These high peaks emptied out into deep valleys that were crisscrossed by narrow passages, dried up river beds, and rocky ravines.

There was something strangely familiar about the topography outlined on that yellowed map, and gazing down at the crinkled surface while running her fingers along the pencil tracings left the reader with strange feelings of recollection and remembrance. Even if one overlooked the apparent age of the chart, it was ridiculous to consider the possibility that any modern day reader could have once crossed such a desert or wandered through those valleys and not remembered. The reader shrugged off her feelings by reasoning that she had once seen such a map in a museum or could merely be recalling it from a childhood story about buried treasure or some other great adventure.

The reader carefully refolded the map along its original lines and tucked it safely back into its hiding place. She could not help but wonder what had caused the author of this diary to leave the comfort of home ,and the fellowship of friends, to set out on the journey that these pencil tracings now marked. Convinced that the diary had mistakenly ended up in the cardboard box of discarded belongings, she flipped back to its front page to look again at the name that was penned there. The pilgrimage detailed in the traveler's map seemed an arduous trip for even the most skilled adventurer and therefore highly unlikely for the rightful owner of these belongings. Surprisingly, the name she found was that of the woman who once valued these now discarded treasures. The discoverer of the diary was even more intrigued by her find as she contemplated what could have prompted an everyday woman much like herself to dare to cross over such seemingly hostile terrain. She wondered what sorts of secrets might have been discovered by the one who penned the diary as she followed her quest and what reward awaited her at journey's end.

The curious reader tingled with delight as she anticipated the possible storehouse of information that would be surrendered up from this discarded little book that was now marked with age and the faint smell of mildew and must. Somehow she knew that the humble and disheveled appearance of that little diary belied the value of the contents carefully shared between the time worn covers. Her heart was beating loudly as she settled down into the library chair. She was hoping that the diary's opening pages might reveal a clue of some long since changed landmark to jostle her memory and settle the ridiculous ,yet nagging, feeling of recollection that was hovering in the back of her mind. The reader secretly fantasized that the writing would also disclose a path to a great treasure of immeasurable wealth hidden somewhere in one of those caves, or buried just beneath the surface of the arid desert sand.

The reader breathed in a deep sigh and carefully grasped the fragile corner of the first onion-skinned page. So began her search to uncover the wealth of treasure that might be awaiting her...*Welcome to this Disciple Daughter's Diary* were the first words to greet her

Introduction

Welcome to *this* disciple daughter's diary. I admit that it does not go without notice that the title of this collection reads a bit like the ritualized warm up exercise of a vocal coach or a frustrated Broadway star. The meter of the title's chosen words does resemble a tongue twister or sound something along the lines of "*Moses supposes his toes are roses*" or "*she sells seashells by the seashore*". I will confess that my writing is prone to the embroidery of alliterative phrasing, sentiment, and poetic hyperbole. In short, I have been told that I am "wordy". But I pray that you will overlook my wordiness and embrace the title that I've chosen as it best describes the contents tucked between the diary's covers and carefully transcribed onto these pages. For what the reader will discover here are indeed the musings, or the random thoughts, ideas, and contemplations of a daughter within God's kingdom who found herself meandering between harsh and dry places while traversing across the sometimes exhausting desert of transition

Readers may likewise find themselves prone to compare some of the thoughts transcribed within these pages to the Biblical account of the Children of Israel as they made their arduous trek through the wilderness. The two accounts are not without similarity. The heavenly Father had intended the wilderness and desert experiences chronicled within this diary as a time to prepare me for ministry, to deepen my knowledge, to strengthen my foundation, and to develop my intimacy with Him. Unfortunately, just as in the story of those wandering Hebrew Children, my time of desert and wilderness too quickly became a time of impatience, frustration, and resentment toward God.

While telling my Father that I trusted His provision as sufficient for my every need I secretly longed to fill my nostrils with the aroma of meat and leeks cooking back home on the grills of Egypt. I quickly rebelled against Him for having taken everything away from me, and then complained that

He had unfairly placed me in too harsh a set of circumstances. It wasn't long after I followed the Shepherd away from the camp that I missed the noise of the crowds and the frivolity of the others dancing around the calf. It would have been impossible to distinguish me from any other member of that traveling tribe as I joined in with the Children of Israel in their all too familiar chorus of whining and complaining. I accused my maker of stripping me and then of leaving me naked and alone to die there in unfamiliar and unwelcoming surroundings

I had repeatedly begged my maker to let me come into His holy presence and to show me His face. Then, as God bid me come join Him on His holy mountain top; I complained at the steepness of the climb. I had gone away in the hopes of hearing from my God, and even as I entered into His chambers, my mind wandered back to the folks at home. I second guessed my spiritual discipline and the depth of my appetite for time spent in solitude. I said that I desired to know the Lord in His completeness, but soon longed for the company of others.

My purpose in openly sharing the devotions, thoughts, prayers, and contemplations contained in this disciple daughter's diary is to encourage and to provoke thought in those readers who may find that their present journey has them traveling through territories similar to those described. I have learned that as we grow in the Lord, each of us is at one point or another called away to join Him in the places that bring piercing pain to the flesh followed by deep and unquenchable thirst in our souls. I have likewise learned that if we truly desire to know our Savior in the power of His glorious resurrection, then our journey must begin, as His did, at the crucifixion. Scripture calls for each of us to crucify our own flesh (Galatians 2:20). As Christ's disciples, we are called by Him to deny ourselves, to take up our cross, and to follow Him obediently wherever He leads (Luke 9:23). The flesh, however, does not go to the cross willingly or die without a fight. The will's struggle for supremacy begins at the moment we determine to work out our salvation with fear and trembling (Philippians 2:12).

Our Father desires to purify us, to refine us, and to grow us up into a closer reflection of Him. This is why He calls for us to move out, to follow Him into a place where we have never been before, and to willingly begin our journey of transition. Obeying our Father's call requires our willingness to leave title, position, and the security of church, home, family, and community behind to faithfully follow where ever the Shepherd leads. The honor of entering into the throne room requires a letting go, a death to self, a willingness to start over, and an earnest desire to obtain all that our loving Father has to offer. The disciple daughter who would dare to follow the Lord's call to come away with Him, and to climb the mount of God to enter into His holy presence, must first submit to His leading and yield to His touch. She must also be willing to forsake all to make the journey alone.

Every disciple daughter's journey begins with high anticipation, absolute obedience, and total abandonment to God's purposes. While it is true that our present day places of soul searching and refinement do not take the form of literal desert or wilderness; these times of questioning and of testing do come just the same. A disciple daughter may quickly discover that as the result of her desire to know Christ, and her attempts to crucify the flesh, she is now wandering through the Valley of Shadows, or stretched to the point of breaking during aimless meandering within dense fogs of confusion and doubt. That Valley of Shadows may be found sitting at the bedside of a terminally-ill loved one. Her Wide Wilderness of Want may appear in the form of a bankruptcy, or through the loss of a business, or a home. Divorce court proceedings may compose the walls of the dark pit of loneliness, rejection, and betrayal in which a disciple daughter now sits trapped as she watches the fogs of confusion and doubt begin to roll in overhead. A rebellious child, an unfaithful spouse, and seemingly countless unanswered prayers may all contribute to the tangled briers and twisted branches of the wilderness thicket that block the sun's warmth and light from the path on which the present day sojourner now travels. Such is the terrain that might be traced on the map of a modern day disciple daughter

Do not be discouraged faithful daughter. The circumstances of your life are designed with purpose. Your Father has heard your pleas to know Him, and has set your course with your heart's cry in mind. He has already traveled the road up ahead which He now lays before you. However hostile or unwelcoming the territory in which you sojourn may seem; you are not abandoned. Every step is ordained. Your Father sees and knows the path that you take. He loves you dearly, and desires only to bless you, and to refine you to a closer reflection of His image. God Almighty longs for you to know Him as sufficient for your every need, and to become the primary relationship of your life. He can work even the meanest circumstances of your life for your good, and to His glory; if you will simply trust and follow His voice.

Rest assured, disciple daughter, that each of the places of solitude, of testing, and of stripping away that you encounter can be transformed into the most precious time of sweet fellowship. They can become a time of blessed dwelling in the presence of the One who loves you as no other. This can only be accomplished by seeking to nurture an intimate relationship with Him above all else. All of life's other cares, desires, and distractions must be tied to the altar and laid at the Father's feet. The minutia of daily life must be trusted to His keeping. Every goal and aspiration must be tested by fire and may as a result be burned as dross. Embarking on this journey will require that the responding disciple daughter lay aside every preconceived notion of her Maker in order to see Him as He really is.

And so our journey begins...

But He knoweth the way that I take; when He hath tried me,
I shall come forth as gold.
Job 23:10

Setting Out in Anticipation

It was early morning when the disciple daughter heard the Shepherd's voice calling out to her. The sun was barely visible over the eastern gate of the city as she collected her bags and stepped out onto the front walkway. Her heart skipped a beat as she pulled the door closed behind her and started down the garden path. She secretly wondered how long it would be before her mother would miss her and questioned whether or not the members of her family would understand her need to leave them behind and embark on this journey without them. She had tried to share her heart with them many times before, but they were settled in their thinking. They were happy with their lives and their careers. It was true that they loved the Shepherd too, but that love had been dimmed by the routines and habits of daily living. Some had cautioned her not to be too zealous and smiled that knowing smile as they patted her shoulder and assured her that soon, she too, would settle down and put her love for the Shepherd in proper perspective with the remainder of her life's affections and duties. Others counseled that it was naïve of her to think that her love for the Shepherd could remain so steadfast and all-consuming for the rest of her days. They suggested that other loves would soon demand her attention and reasoned that she was still young; maturity and the difficult experiences of life would quickly quell her zest and excitement. Smiling to herself, the disciple daughter decided that while all of this might be true at some point, it certainly wasn't true today. She could hardly catch her breath as she hurried out the gate and down the dusty road. Young or not, she knew that she was about to set out on the adventure of a lifetime. The lover of her soul had invited her to come away with Him and she was finally ready to accept His invitation. She felt especially blessed to have been chosen as His travel companion on this incredible journey.

The disciple daughter's anticipation grew with each step. She could practically hear her heart beating in her ears, because she knew that her friend would be waiting just outside the city gates in their secret meeting place. From the beginning of their relationship, she had always made it her practice to get up early every morning to spend time with Him before the hectic pace of her day could steal away her time. She valued the advice that He offered and enjoyed starting each day being reminded of His great love for her. His presence seemed to calm her spirit and dispel all her fears. She could not help but be at peace whenever she was near Him.

As the excited sojourner traveled out of the city and beyond the gates, her mind wandered back to recall happy times spent in the Shepherd's presence since early childhood. They had carefully studied the Father's Word together and she had learned to plant all of His precepts and commandments deeply within her heart. She greatly enjoyed their time together and always waited in anticipation for each meeting as she knew He would be bringing her good gifts directly from His Father's hand. Her teacher never seemed too busy for her and encouraged her to come to Him with all her questions and concerns. He never failed to answer any time she called and often told her that His Father had no greater joy than watching her grow and begin to walk in His truth.

Later, as their relationship deepened, the disciple daughter felt honored that the Father had allowed her to draw so closely to Him. He ushered her freely into His throne room and opened up to her about the secret things of His kingdom. She began to understand His ways as well as to trust His character. She also learned many things about the Father simply by watching the mannerisms and habits of her Shepherd and friend. She felt as if she knew her Father's heart and was confident of His desires and ability to perform His will regarding her. The Shepherd moved in gentleness and patience toward her and seemed to honestly take joy in fellowshipping with her. She never parted from His presence without feeling deeply loved and favored as His disciple and partner in fulfilling the Father's business.

The disciple daughter had been particularly busy at home in the most recent years, carrying out the Father's business and obeying all that He had instructed. She was teaching others within her own community as well as in nearby towns about how to walk in the freedom of the Father's truth. The disciple daughter desired to live a life that pleased her Father and took great care to walk in a manner that was worthy of His great love. She wanted her Father to have full confidence in her obedience and found great joy in fulfilling His will and honoring His name among His people. She was honored to have an assignment as the ambassador of His kingdom. He was her Father, the King, and the one from whom every good gift originated. She recognized the high privilege of a call to His service and prayed that her actions would reflect His great love because she wanted others to know and to love Him as she knew and loved Him.

The vision that the Father had recently opened up to her required risk taking and great faith. The LORD Himself had initiated an invitation for her to come away to commune together with His Son and with Him on His holy mountain. The Father explained that her time with Him in His throne room would require that she leave family and home and be willing to make the difficult trek across unchartered land to meet with Him alone. He would not provide her with a compass or a map; He wanted her to make her way by relying upon the precepts and truths that she had stored in her heart. Her only light would be the small lantern that He would provide to illuminate each step along her ordained path. Of course, she would have the full assurance of the Shepherd's company as well as His rod and staff to protect and comfort her.

The Father explained that the purpose of this journey was to prepare His ambassador for new ministry, expanded territory, and greater service. He wanted the disciple daughter to understand from the onset that accepting this new mantle would require total surrender to His will and purpose for her life. He reminded the traveler of His promise to supply all of her needs as they were presented to Him, but cautioned that she would need to trust Him as her sufficiency because she would be allowed to pack only minimal provisions. The disciple daughter's security would have to be firmly anchored in the Father's promises, as there would be times of great testing and stretching that He would allow along the way. He asked His disciple daughter to carefully consider the costs should she decide to commit to the trip ahead. He was giving her complete freedom of choice and of will.

The disciple daughter's excitement could not be dampened. She assured the Father that she had counted the costs and had no fear. She was totally secure in His great love and knew that the Good Shepherd would lead her out while the Holy Spirit would be there to guide and to encourage. She would not be dismayed and could not imagine feeling alone or abandoned for even a second as long as she was traveling in their company. She fully trusted the details of the trip to her Father's care, because she knew of His great love and concern for His own. The disciple daughter reasoned that such a life-changing opportunity was worth any price.

Her friend and teacher was not slack concerning His promises to her. She saw Him waiting just ahead in the early morning light. He said that He would come for her, and He did. The Shepherd called out to her by name and extended His arm as He beckoned her to come alongside. That same great arm that made the earth and sustains all life upon it was now outstretched lovingly toward her. The disciple daughter knew that she would set out on this journey secured by His great strength and comforted by His mighty hand. The Good Shepherd would guide her safely into the Father's holy dwelling place. She ran to Him and could hardly contain her joy. The Shepherd smiled down at her, slipped His arm lovingly around her waist and guided her down the path that the Father had set before them. The two set out side by side. The disciple daughter and the lover of her soul were going away meet with the King of Kings. She was *thrilled*!

Walking as the Daughters of the King

Scripture Meditation

"What, then, shall we say in response to this? If God is for us, who can be against us?"(Romans 8:31).

"The heavens declare the glory of God; the skies proclaim the work of his hands"(Psalm 19:1).

"What agreement is there between the temple of God and idols? For we are the temple of the living God. As God has said: '"I will live with them and walk among them, and I will be their God, and they will be my people'."(2 Corinthians 6:16).

Musing

Sadly, many disciple daughters do not have a positive association with God as "our Father" because they've had strained or difficult relationships with their earthly fathers. Their definition of the word "father" has been colored by past experiences. If they've had relationships that are marked by mistrust, abuse, neglect, or distance with their earthly fathers then they may now have a hard time believing what the Bible has to say about the character attributes and habits of their heavenly Father. This God of whom the Bible speaks is described as being majestic in holiness and as lacking nothing. He is awesome in glory, unfailing in love, and all powerful. His resources are unlimited and no other being's deeds can compare to His marvelous works. He is the one who brings out the starry host and then calls each one by name as He tells it where to stand within His universe. He alone sits enthroned on high, and the whole world declares His glory (Psalm 19).

The above description might be a little intimidating or difficult for us to completely comprehend. It is impossible for a finite mind to grasp the character of a being who is infinite. It is even more difficult to believe that any being with attributes such as those described above would want anything to do with anyone as insignificant as one of us . Yet, the single most significant and awe inspiring characteristic of God is His great love (1 John 4:8). As a matter of fact, God wants us to know that His love for us is unconditional. He loved us so much that He sent His Son, Jesus Christ, to die for us while we were still unlovable sinners (Romans 5:8, John 3:16,Ephesians1:4-10). Making us His daughters was God's idea and was compelled by His great love. We didn't have to clean up our act, perform to His standards, wait until we were better suited or strike any negotiations with God before we could experience His love. He loved us before we knew Him. Our adoption was His plan and He did all the giving and sacrificing to set that plan into motion (Ephesians 1:4-10).The good news that I want to share as we start out on our journey to becoming all that God intended for each of us to be is that regardless of what your relationship with your earthly father is or was, now, through the blood sacrifice of Jesus Christ, we can all have an eternal relationship with the Father of every little girl's dreams!

As daughters of the Kings of Kings we are wholly accepted and unconditionally loved . We are eternally held in His strong arms. Ephesians 1:3-5 says that our Father chose us before the foundations of the earth. He adopted us for His good pleasure and His love for us is everlasting; therefore we have no need for feelings of inadequacy. Our Father finds great joy and pleasure in us. The Prophet Zephaniah says that He expresses His love over us with sweet songs of tender love. (Psalm 104, Zephaniah 3:14, 17). He sees us as perfect through the blood sacrifice of His beloved Son Jesus and we are a showcase of His strength and beauty. Christ's love has redeemed us from all curses. His love will never fail us. Even if the mountains and hills disappear, our Father's faithful love will remain (Isaiah 54:10). The Word of God has settled that (Psalm119:89). Our Father is not fickle or frivolous concerning His promises (Isaiah49:15, Malachi 3:6). God is who He says He is and He will do what He says that He will do.

As daughters of the King we do not need to worry about being rejected or being concerned that our Father will be too busy or unavailable to us. We have direct access to the throne room of *The* God above all gods. On the day that we were adopted into the family of God through the blood of Jesus Christ our identity shifted, our names changed, and we were no longer excluded from citizenship or considered as foreigners to the covenant of God's promise (Ephesians 2:12). We are new creations, children of God, and joint heirs of His kingdom (2 Corinthians 5:17, Romans 8:17). We now have the right to call God our *"Abba-Father" (*Romans *8:15-16).* That word *Abba* means "Daddy". The right to use that name is only given to those who carry the last name of God Almighty and are therefore rightful heirs. All of heaven recognizes us as His daughters and has been instructed not to bar us from our Father's throne room. It is true that our God is the everlasting *I AM* and equally true that He is our *Abba-Daddy.* As His daughters we have unhindered fellowship with the God of the universe and can run right into the throne room of our *Abba-Father* (Hebrews 4:16). It is there in His throne room that we will find limitless resources and unending power that has been made available by our Heavenly Father to meet our needs. The only limitations the daughters of the king have are those that we place upon God or those that result from our unwillingness to ask of Him.

Our Heavenly Father desires to lavish upon us. Scripture teaches that we have all that we need and the desires of our hearts are met through Him. All of God's promises have been fulfilled in Christ with a resounding *Yes!* for His children (2 Corinthians 1: 20). We can rest in the assurance from Scripture that if we trust the Lord and surrender our lives to His keeping, He will give us the desires of our heart. Our Father has supplied all that we need to represent Him while traveling here on this earth. He promises to fill our mouths full when we open them to Him (Psalm 81:10). We can't even possibly begin to comprehend all the wonderful things that our Father has in store for those who love Him (1 Corinthians 2:9).

As daughters of the King we have a hope and a future. Our lives have a purpose and we are being changed into vessels that are perfectly equipped to do all that our Father has in mind for us to accomplish (Ephesians 2:10). Our Father's plans are motivated by His great love for us. He desires to bless us and to prosper us. He would never wish us any harm. God promises that when we call to Him, He will answer us and give us His full attention (Jeremiah 29:11-14).

We also have great hope in the fact that we are being transformed from glory to glory as we submit to our Father's design plans and to His creative power (2 Corinthians 5:17). Sometimes, because we are a work in progress, we may not see the outcome of our Father's plan. We can rest assured, however, that He does have one for each of us. We can also take comfort knowing that our Father does not faint or grow weary and that His understanding is unsearchable (Isaiah 40:28-29). If our Father doesn't grow weary with us or give up on our potential then neither should we. We need to be gracious to ourselves and to have patience with our seemingly slow advancement.

We inherit our royal status, our new last name, and our robes of righteousness at the moment of adoption into the family of God, but then we must grow up into the authority of our newly inherited position. We learn how to put on our robes, claim our inheritance, carry the attitude of a king's daughter, and walk in our authority much like we learn how to move with elegance and grace in a pair of high heels. Our walk may be awkward at first and we may stumble and falter. We can be encouraged by remembering that we are co-laborers together with God in this process. It is God, through the person of His Holy Spirit, who does the transforming. The process of change is initiated by the Holy Spirit as we surrender our life to His control and learn to be sensitive to His leading. Steadfastly trusting in Him and leaning on His truth will steady our steps.

How big is your God, daughter of the King? How much do you believe and claim what He has to say about you and about His plans for you? Have you claimed your birthright of lavish love, magnanimous grace, magnificent mercy, eternal life and joy unspeakable? Are you looking to your maker as the source of peace that passes all understanding? Are you allowing His rivers of living water to flow through you to sustain, refresh and renew your soul as you begin your journey across this Desert of Transition? Are you ready to learn how to live as the daughter of the King of Kings?

Heart's Cry

God, you are my God. There is no other god in heaven on or earth with which to compare you. Teach me what it means to be your daughter and help me to embrace all the wonderful truth of who you are. Secure my steps as I anchor my identity in you. My heart's desire is to know you and to love you with all that I am and ever will be. Amen

Walking with the Shepherd

Scripture Meditation

"The Lord is my Shepherd, I shall not want. He makes me lie down in green pastures, he leads me beside quiet waters, and he restores my soul. He leads me in the paths of righteousness for his names' sake. Even though I walk through the valley of the shadow of death, I will fear no evil, for you are with me, your rod and your staff they comfort me. You prepare a table before me in the presence of my enemies. You anoint my head with oil; my cup overflows. Surely goodness and love will follow me all the days of my life and I will dwell in the house of the LORD forever."(Psalm 23).

"God is our refuge and strength, an ever present help in trouble. Therefore we will not fear, though the earth gives way and the mountains fall into the heart of the sea, though its waters roar and foam, and the mountains quake with their surging"(Psalm 46:1-3).

"The man who enters by the gate is the shepherd of his sheep. The watchman opens the gate for him and the sheep listen to his voice. He calls his own sheep by name and leads them out. When he has brought out all his own, he goes ahead of them and his sheep follow him because they know his voice."(John 10:2-4).

"I am the good shepherd; I know my sheep and my sheep know me- just as the Father knows me and I know the Father- and I lay down my life for the sheep."(John 10:14-15).

Musing

There is a certain pace or rhythm in walking with the Lord. He does not tug at us or keep us tightly reined under His control. It is also true, perhaps to our chagrin that our Shepherd will never pick us up and carry us when we rebelliously refuse to budge or to go with Him as He directs. Neither will He force His desires upon us or drag us unwillingly behind Him. He leads us by His gentle calling. He goes out ahead of us and bids us to come and to follow (John 10:2-4).We must decide for ourselves upon hearing His voice whether we will go where and as He directs (Ephesians 5:15-16, Philippians 1:27). The sheep of the Shepherd follow of their own free will. The path that they take is always of their own volition.

If we wish to choose wisely and to follow obediently, then, as the Lord's sheep, we must listen and discern carefully. There will be many voices speaking myriad different messages to us as we travel our life's pathway. It will be important that we know which voice is His and we must be careful to follow only where that voice leads. We must learn to sense His pace and to feel His cadence; to be still when He leads us to lie down and to trust His sovereign wisdom and perfect timing (Psalm23:2, Lamentations 3:26, Jeremiah 29:10-11). Though our Shepherd promises to offer protection when the thief or the wolf threaten us; we must keep our eyes focused on His footsteps and be cautiously aware of our enemy's tactics (John 10:12-13, 1 Peter 5:8). Our Shepherd assures us that He will keep us from stumbling and our feet from being caught in the snare (Psalm 24:15, Psalm 37:23-24). He will also freely lay down His life to rescue us (John 10:15). However, in order to receive His promises we must stay within His hedges of protection and abide within the safety of His folds.

As the Good Shepherd's sheep, we can follow without fear even as we sojourn along treacherous pathways and cross through valleys filled with shadows and darkness (Psalm 23:4). He knows us by name and His great love will guide and protect us (John 10:3, Psalm 23:4-6). He promises to be our help in times of trouble and to provide refuge in times of peril (Psalm 46:1-3, 54:4). We can be confident that our Shepherd knows what is best for us and will provide all that we need as we place our lives in His care (Philippians 4:4-6, Psalm 23:2, 5). We can be content whether we are traveling through lush green meadows or over harsh wilderness and rocky terrain that what our Shepherd lovingly provides will be our sufficiency (Philippians 4:11-12, 2 Corinthians 12:9). Everything that He does is motivated by His great compassion, goodness, mercy and love for each of His sheep (Psalm 23:6, John 10:14).

The Lord is good to those whose hope is in Him and to those who seek Him (Lamentations 3:2). His goodness and mercy will fill our lives to overflowing and we will forever abide in His presence and under His watchful care if we choose to follow His leading (Psalm 23:6, Matthew 28:18-20, Romans 8:38). He remembers His covenant forever and is faithful to all His promises (Psalm 104:8).

Heart's Cry

Father God, I desire to start out every morning as your sheep listening for your voice and discerning your direction for my life. Teach me to commit myself to your care and to rest contently in your provision. Give me assurance when I am insecure or frightened by causing me to remember your great love and compassion as my Good Shepherd. Increase my discernment and help me to be watchful in every step as I follow you without hesitation. Amen

Intimacy with God

Oh that my soul's desire would be to know God.
To be utterly lifted from this natural plain into His holy presence…
To be transfixed by His glory and to gaze with unmasked face into His eyes.
To fall down in worship at His Throne;
to kiss His feet as I anoint them with my tears and wipe them with my hair.
Oh, for a span of time measured by eternity to praise Him,
To lift voices in your honor and to exalt your holy name.
Such a time would not be time enough.
For you alone are worthy.
You are altogether lovely and altogether beautiful.
My Maker,
My Master,
My Redeemer,
My Savior,
My Sovereign,
My King.
Hallelujah to Jehovah.

Separation unto the Lord

Scripture Meditation

"Who may ascend the hill of the LORD? Who may stand in his holy place? He who has clean hands and a pure heart, who does not lift up his soul to an idol or swear by what is false. He will receive blessing from the LORD and vindication from God his Savior."(Psalm 24:3-5).

"Blessed are the pure in heart, for they shall see God' (Matthew 5:8).

"In bringing many sons to glory, it was fitting that God, for whom and through whom everything exists, should make the author of their salvation perfect through suffering. Both the one who makes men holy and those who are made holy are of the same family. So Jesus is not ashamed to call them brothers."(Hebrews2:10-11).

"Enter through the narrow gate. For wide is the gate and broad is the road that leads to destruction, and many enter through it. But small is the gate and narrow the road that leads to life and only a few find it. (Matthew 7:13-14).

Musing

There comes a point in the life of each disciple who sincerely desires to follow Christ above all else when she must choose to separate herself from those who do not share that same desire or her same level of intensity and urgency. This separation may not be limited to non-believers but may also include those within the Body of Christ who are content to remain where they are or who do not desire a deeper, more mature walk with the Lord. Seeking to exhibit Christlikeness and holiness in our lives by refusing to love the world or the things of it will require that we make God's will and His kingdom principles a priority and the standard for our daily conduct. Our commitment to true discipleship will require a personal decision to enter into God's presence and to separate from those who have not made the same choices. This may mean that we go on ahead without our friends and family members for a season.

As believers under the new covenant of today , when we speak of ascending the holy hill of God, we are speaking of Mount Zion rather than of Mount Sinai (Psalm 24,Isaiah 8:18). Mount Sinai was important to the people of faith in the Old Testament because it was the mountain upon which God gave Moses His covenant for the people of Israel. It was the mountain that Moses temporarily ascended into God's presence. Mount Sinai was the mountain of the law. Contrarily, Mount Zion, which is the holy hill of the New Testament, is the mount of grace rather than of law and it is the eternal dwelling place of God (Hebrews 12:18-24). The entrance gates to this holy hill are opened by Jesus alone. Access is freely granted to all who have trusted in His gift of redemption. He is the only true gatekeeper or the true door of the flock (John 10:7).Christ is the only doorway and disciples desiring to approach the presence of God on His holy hill can only do so by first going by the way of another hill. That hill is *Calvary*.

The good news for those of us who approach Holy God through His new covenant entrance is that God provides everything that we need through the person of Jesus Christ and His mighty work of redemption. God is still a holy God and no sinner can ascend into His holy hill; but now absolute, perfect, undefiled righteousness is ours through the sacrifice of Jesus Christ (Hebrews 10:1-12). Through Christ we have total access to the presence of God. His sacrifice has purchased our admission. Hallelujah!

Moses went up Mount Sinai unaccompanied when he met with God. Likewise, we cannot ascend God's holy hill or know the fullness of His abiding presence as long as we desire the company of those who are carnally minded or unwilling to yield in obedience to the will of God for their lives. Our Maker desires fellowship and intimacy with us but He will not share the throne of our will or our heart with false gods, religious rituals and legalisms, or idols. The idols that are most commonly found within the lives of New Testament disciples would include anything that is deemed "more important", of greater value, or "more pressing" than giving our complete worship and the total abandon of our will and wants to the obedient service of the one true God. He will not share our time or our devotion with other causes or loves (Revelation 2:1-7). If we would meet with Him on His holy hill then we must acknowledge Him as the only true God and as the sovereign of our life. Seeking to worship God in any other fashion is contrary to His covenant and will not be blessed. It is not enough that Yahweh; the God of Abraham, Isaac and Jacob, be worshiped along with other deities. We are to abandon anything and anyone that gets in the way of our relationship with, and worship of, the one true God. As followers of Christ we are called to willingly crucify all desires and affections that derive from our flesh (Galatians 2:20).

As our propitiation and scapegoat, Jesus suffered outside the camp to make us holy and to establish our righteousness before God (Hebrews 13:11). He now asks that we be willing to come outside the camp to meet Him and then be willing to forsake the fellowship of others for the opportunity of fellowshipping with Him (Exodus 32:22-25). If we are to know God in His fullness then we must be willing to put away our childish pastimes and begin the process of maturing in the faith (1 Corinthians 13:11, Hebrews 5:12-14). An unobstructed view of God in His complete holiness; high and lifted up upon His throne, is only possible for those who have erected no idols or other barriers between themselves and His presence (Isaiah 6:1-4). He alone is worthy of all our praise and worship for He is the one true God (Psalm 145:3, Isaiah 44:6).

Heart's Cry

Forsaking all, Lord, I choose you. Help me to avoid becoming lazy or complacent and to continue to inherit what has been promised to me through your covenant. I desire to enter into the inner sanctuary and then on into the holy of holies found beyond the veil to meet you and to worship you in view of your full glory. Help me Father to stop wasting time and to go on from here as I discipline myself to desire your life giving truth above all else. Amen

Calling Jesus "Friend"

Scripture Meditation

"When Jesus came to the region of Caesarea Philippi, he asked his disciples, "Who do people say the Son of Man is?" They replied, "Some say John the Baptist, other say Elijah; and still others, Jeremiah or one of the prophets." "But what about you?" He asked. "Who do you say I am?"(Matthew 16:13-14).

"You are my friends if you do what I command. I No longer call you servants because a servant does not know his master's business. Instead, I have called you friends, for everything that I learned from my Father I have made known to you."(John 15:14-15).

"But if anyone obeys his word, God's love is truly made complete in him. This is how we know we are in him: Whoever claims to live in him must walk as Jesus did."(1 John 2:5-6).

"You adulterous people, don't you know that friendship with the world is hatred toward God? Anyone who chooses to be a friend of the world becomes an enemy of God."(James 4:4).

Musing

The manner in which we conduct our daily living hinges directly upon our answer to the very same question that Jesus posed to His disciples in Matthew 16: 14. Jesus wanted to know who these men who were traveling with Him had come to believe Him to be. Others who had seen Jesus or who may have gathered to hear His teaching identified Him as a good man, a worker of miracles and in some cases as one of the prophets. Jesus now asked His disciples what they would choose to call Him and who they claimed He was. What Jesus was actually asking of His disciples was for them to define their relationship with Him because He knew that the answer that they gave to His simple question would determine how much influence, priority and authority He would be allowed within their individual and corporate lives.

In John 15:14 Jesus identifies only those who do what He commands as His friends. Repeatedly scripture teaches that following God's commandments and adhering to Jesus' teaching is how we demonstrate our love for Him and model His love to the world (John 14:15, 21, 23-24, 1 John 2:3-6).Scripture also warns that disobedience to His Word or compromising His instructions is the equivalent of adultery or to the act of being unfaithful to a sacred covenant relationship (James 4:4). Clearly, if we are going to be identified as a friend of Jesus, then regardless of present circumstances or the current situation of our life, the authority of Jesus' teachings must be absolute.

Obedience to His teaching and the willingness to follow His commands are the foundational requirements to being friends with Jesus (John 15:14). If two sojourners desire to be traveling partners for any distance then both must agree upon their route and their destination. Logic dictates that two people moving in opposite directions cannot travel together. One traveler may even need to change her direction or alter her route if the two wish to walk in agreement. Likewise, anyone seeking to be friends with God and to establish an intimate relationship with Him cannot be in an intimate friendship with anyone or anything that leaves Him out or stands in opposition to His teaching (John 3:19-20). Having such affections sets our course in opposite direction to God's will for us. Scripture teaches that being a friend of the world and/ or its values, perspectives and views puts us at odds with our maker and our redeemer (James 1:27, 4:4). We cannot continue to fellowship with or to set our affections for the things of this world and remain in right relationship with our Lord (1 John 5:19).

Friendships take time to develop and are cultivated through the sharing of such things as our hopes, aspirations, life goals and objectives. Notice that Jesus explained that the difference between those whom He identified as *a servant* and those whom He now called *a friend* was that a friend knows his master's business (John 15:14-15). Jesus told His disciples that He had cultivated His friendship with them by sharing everything that He had learned from His Father (John 15:15). He also explained in the very next verse of this same passage that He chose us as His friends; we did not choose Him (John 15:16). How should we respond to the truth that Jesus first initiated the opportunity for our friendship with Him and then freely shared all that He is, has and knows with anyone desiring such a relationship? If it is true that He has freely shared all that His Father shared with Him then as His friends we should take the time necessary to search out and to know the details of the business He has shared. As Jesus' co-heirs and friends we must dedicate ourselves to carrying on His Father's business in His absence. We must do things as He would until He returns again from His Father. As Jesus' friends and co-heirs we have the responsibility to take up our Father's business and to spread Jesus' teachings around the world (Luke 2:49, Mathew 28:18-20).

How do we answer the question that Jesus posed to His disciples when He poses it to us today? Who do we declare Christ to be? It has been said that actions speak louder than words. Our actions and manner of living reflect the intimacy level of our relationship with Christ and the value that we place upon Him. We may live a life that demonstrates that of an intimate friendship with the Son of God; or one that indicates that Christ is nothing more to us than a moral man, a good teacher, a prophet of the Bible, or a carpenter's son who worked miracles. Whoever we are, whatever we do, whatever the current circumstances of our lives, our daily conduct should be different if we profess that Jesus is our friend. His level of influence and authority should be priority in our lives as individuals as well as within the corporate body of believers if we desire to model our friendship with Him to the world. We should be about the Father's business because it was entrusted to our keeping by our friend.

Heart's Cry

What a high and holy privilege to be called the friend of God! Father, help me to live out my life in a manner that exemplifies that title. Give me the desire to search out the truth and the discipline needed to actualize your teachings in my daily interaction with others as well as with you. Help me to recognize what great love you lavished on me by counting me righteous and then calling me your child and your friend. As your heir, help me to bring you honor and glory as I seek to accomplish the business of your kingdom until you return. Amen.

Direction

Direct my Path Sweet Shepherd Divine,
As I yield my control and trust completely in Thine.
My Hopes and dreams are now placed in your hands alone.
The center of my will make now thy throne."

Trusting Our Advocate

Scripture Meditation

"Thine ear shall hear a word behind thee, saying, this is the way, walk ye in it, when ye turn to the right hand, and when ye turn to the left"(Isaiah 30:21).

"Therefore since we have a great high priest who has gone through the heavens, Jesus the Son of God, let us hold firmly to the faith that we profess. For *we do not have* a high priest who is unable to sympathize with our weaknesses *but we have one* who has been tempted in every way just as we are- yet without sin. Let us approach the throne of grace with confidence so that we may receive mercy and find grace to help us in our time of need."(*Hebrews 4:14-16*).

Musing

Strap on your sandals and follow your Shepherd (Acts 12:8). Rest in the assurance that you know His voice though many other voices may advise and urge you otherwise. Remember that we walk by faith and not by appearance (2 Corinthians 5:7). Faith is our evidence when there is no other sign. Faith is our security even when we are strangers in a harsh foreign land.

Our Father wants us to leave the details and desires of earthly living to His care and to simply follow in childlike faith. That faith will be tested with delays, with suffering, with heartache and with a stretching, perhaps to the point of being certain that we will break. Faith must believe unwavering through every phase of our journey and across every terrain in which we travel that God will keep His covenant and provide His promised blessing.

Should we stumble or falter and fail to keep our faith securely focused on the truth of God's Word we can rest in the knowledge that we have a loving and caring Savior . Jesus is our advocate, redeemer, intercessor and friend. He is also our guarantee of full access to the throne room of God where we can find all that we need and desire. He invites us to come with our imperfections and short-comings and there to find righteousness and atonement through Him.

Our enemy desires nothing more than to keep us from doing exactly what our Lord beckons us to do in these moments of failure and doubt. Satan desires to keep us defeated and in despair because he knows that a dispirited disciple will not push forward and will grow faint out in the desert or wilderness alone. He also knows what power can be ours and the grace, love, forgiveness and peace we will find waiting for us if we will only come as God's child and repent. That is precisely why he wants to keep us bound up, weighed down and discouraged in the weight of our sin and short comings. Faith will not be activated without surrender and surrender cannot co-exist with a heart that is sinful or a will that is unrepentant. Our enemy knows that coming to the Father with a prayer of repentance will only free us and allow us to do greater things in the Lord's name.

Jesus has already gone to the cross for us. He fully paid the price required to satisfy the penalty of our sin. He has made restitution and provided a way into the inner chambers for us by His merit alone. He now waits for us to come in repentance to be forgiven and restored and to receive the answer that we seek. When we repent and enter into the throne room of grace we find that our High Priest is there to make up the difference and to balance our account. He has written our names on His palms. He intercedes on our behalf. Jesus is praying for you, disciple daughter (John 17:20-23). He desires that you be brought to complete unity with His father and know His great love. Do not tarry or stand far off. Come to your Father in confident faith. He always supplies grace and mercy . He always restores and forgives. He loves you so.

Heart's Cry

Father, forgive me for doubting your great love for me. Urge me by the power of your Holy Spirit to always come to you rather than is stand far off in the shame of my sin. Give me eyes to see you and the will to follow you where you lead. Grant me victory over my enemy and do not allow him to trip me or to cause me to falter from my position and course. Amen

The Desert of Transition

The disciple daughter was joyfully making her way along the appointed path with the Shepherd. The days spent in His presence basking in His undivided attention seemed too good to be true. They were sweet beyond measure. She hardly noticed the passage of time or the distance they covered each day as they spent most of their time in deep, personal conversation. The disciple daughter also realized that she wasn't the least bit homesick even though she could no longer see the flicker of the lights from home off in the distance. She understood that pressing toward the prize of the high calling required that she choose to leave the people and places that she loved behind. She had willingly decided to obediently surrender to the Father's call. Time spent previously communing with the Shepherd had taught her that discipleship almost always includes a season of being set apart or of being called away; of surrendering all to follow where the Shepherd leads. She felt that she knew what to expect of the journey that awaited.

While still at home, the disciple daughter made it her practice to rise early each morning in anticipation of quiet time spent in the Lord's presence. She knew that it was important to connect with Him before setting out for the day's assignments. She recalled numerous examples throughout the Bible of those in service to the Lord being called to a time of intense prayer, or of testing and refinement before being launched into greater ministry. She recognized that her call to come away was a great honor and she counted herself among the ranks of prestigious company. Christ reminded her that even He had spent time in the wilderness before entering into His earthly ministry. She had considered the costs as the Shepherd had advised. She was now anxious to prove her faith to Him. She set out on her journey with the Shepherd in great anticipation of the wonderful and mysterious things that would to be opened up to her.

The beginning days of the journey were filled with times of sharing and of joyous conversation. There were also moments of wide eyed astonishment as the Shepherd showed His eager follower new things that had previously been hidden to her. Being alone in His presence without distraction allowed her to more fully understand things that she had not previously comprehended. This wide new place was filled astonishing colors and the night sky practically burst at the seams with stars and planets. Each day spent walking amidst those colors and each night spent gazing up at that sky provided an opportunity to learn and to reflect upon the magnitude of God's creation. The disciple daughter arose each morning eager to see what the Shepherd would reveal on that day's leg of the journey. She recalled the days of Moses and marveled at the fact that she was journeying with the same Shepherd that had led Moses and his people across their desert and through that great sea. The same Holy Spirit was her guide and it was the same right arm securing her that once divided those waters before the Children of Israel. It was easy for her to yield obediently to the Shepherd when she recalled it was His majestic voice that spoke all things into creation.

Too soon the daughter's journey grew longer than anticipated and her life rhythm seemed to slowly devolve into an endless cycle of days in which the sun set and the moon rose across this desert of transition. The sand seemed to have grown thicker and slaving her way through it became much more difficult. It appeared almost alive as it shifted and twisted under her feet; causing her stride to be slightly off balance and keeping her ankles unsteady. It was almost impossible to get a grip on the sand and its blistering heat seemed to burn up through the soles of her sandals. At times just remaining upright through the thick slush proved an arduous physical task. The disciple daughter also had to be on guard for sand traps and quick mire. She had been forewarned that the desert's surface would offer little evidence of one of those deep pits waiting to swallow up an unaware passerby. The sun's rays showed little mercy as they burned down upon her head. The Shepherd would allow her to rest when the heat would become too intense. He'd usher her to a spot near some thorn bushes or scrub brush and offer her a drink of cool water. It was nice to stop and to quench her thirst with the water that the Shepherd so lovingly provided even if the scantily distributed desert vegetation provided little to no shade.

Days passed by far too slowly in this place of shifting sands. The long stretches of never changing landscape and time spent in the intense desert heat were beginning to take their toll. The disciple daughter was growing weary and began to ask her Shepherd when these days of traveling through transition would end. She wanted to know when she would arrive at her destination. She knew that completing her transition successfully would require that she faithfully commit her steps to her Shepherd's keeping whether her journey was spent in singing and dancing, or in heartache and tears; but the disciple daughter now confessed that she longed for human companionship and conversations from home. The wearied traveler was having a difficult time keeping her spirits up with the absence of laughter or the companionship of other travelers. Earlier in her trip she would at least enjoy the company of other pilgrims sojourning through the same area. Her path sometimes crossed with that of a passing caravan or a band of merchants in route to market. The disciple daughter could get news of home and catch up on the latest happenings as they shared a leg of their journey. She resolved to continue on her journey and obediently followed the Shepherd but secretly began to long for the comforts of home and for the greener pastures that she had left behind. Leaving the familiar to face the unknown had left her feeling disconnected and suffering a deep sense of loss. She also hadn't fully anticipated how small and insignificant she would feel traveling amidst this wide and never ending sea of sand. It was as if the desert might swallow her up with her next step and she would disappear forever.

The disciple daughter allowed her mind to wander back to the day she excitedly packed her bags and agreed to join the Shepherd on this journey. She had no idea then that so much of her time would be occupied with traipsing across hot desert sand. She remembered the great anticipation and wonder that once filled her to overflowing. She questioned where that exuberance had gone. Her joyous anticipation was now sometimes overshadowed by fear or dread as she contemplated where it was that the King of the universe would finally send her. She didn't want to believe that her wiser and more settled relatives could be right in their suggestion that her zeal would soon level off. After all, these were extenuating circumstances. It seemed that she had no sooner rounded the corner of her neighborhood than the disciple daughter found herself in a place of driest desert and experiencing a time of extreme testing and stretching. Surely anyone enduring what the Shepherd was asking her to endure would have the same reaction. Such harsh circumstances would be difficult for anyone to bear. She was lonely and lost. She felt as if she was wandering aimlessly, void of compass, map or chart to guide her steps. The Lord had promised that He would not give her more than she could endure but it now seemed that He had forgotten that He had formed her from the dust of the earth.

The heaviness of her footsteps in the sand began to weigh upon the pilgrim. She pleaded with the Shepherd much more often to be allowed to stop and to rest. She was sunburned and tired. Her parched skin was dry and leathered and her soul cried out for a quick dip in the waters of a desert oasis or for the cooling midst of a light rain. The desert was also beginning to tax her faith. She found it troubling that someone could actually feel so lonely while traveling in the company of the Good Shepherd. The disciple knew that she sincerely desired to develop a more intimate relationship with her Father but longed for someone human with whom to share all the wonderful new things that she was learning. The sluggish sojourner tried to strengthen her feeble knees by remembering the Father's earlier warning that her pilgrimage would include times of testing. She wanted to be counted as faithful, so she traveled on; all the while praying that the desert times would soon end and that the Shepherd would quickly lead her out of the heat and dryness of this place and into the Father's holy dwelling.

The section of the desert in which she and the Shepherd were now traveling seemed more desolate and less frequently sojourned by others. The emptiness of her surroundings caused the disciple daughter to be more aware of her need to fix her focus and to keep her bearings. She secretly worried that if she did stop and lose sight of the Shepherd for even one moment she would never find her way out of this dry and isolated desert. She missed the interaction with passing caravans and caught herself often looking for signs of other travelers moving far off in the distance.

It had become impossible for the disciple daughter to measure her progress through the Desert of Transition. There was no way to gain a proper perspective for how far she had come and how far she had yet to go because the desert environment provided no real landmarks. Except for the occasional scrub brush or boulder or rock jutting up from the sand's surface, the scenery around her seemed to never change. It was dull, dry, lifeless and harsh. The disciple daughter considered it miraculous that any life could exist within such a harsh environment.

Wearied and worn to the point of exhaustion, she prayed for the Father to show Himself and to assure her that her journey was almost over. It was true that she wanted to be enlarged in faith and to grow in her knowledge of the Father. It was equally true that she wanted to know the full meaning of all His great promises and desired to be refined into a vessel fit for His service; but deep within her parched soul she longed to be newly inspired by the King's transforming presence. The once wide eyed traveler was no longer excited over the possibility of new discoveries and new assignments. She felt herself procrastinating and overwhelmed by the immenseness of this task. A part of her wanted to turn around and to give up. Perhaps the Father would understand if she simply explained that His call was too great for her at this time. She would assure Him that she would be willing to try again later. Right now her entire being ached and she felt as if she were being weighed down with the weight of a dozen wet and sandy blankets. She was weary and sun parched and just about to throw herself down in the desert sand to be swallowed up in surrender when she caught a glimpse of the Shepherd's hem blowing in the dust as it was being kicked up beneath His feet. Watching Him walk across that unstable and hostile sand as if it were soft, springy earth beneath His feet returned her to determination. She would shake off those overwhelming feelings of defeat and doggedly continue faithfully forward. She knew that she had to focus on her Shepherd and make Him the standard that would inform her progress rather than measure her forward success against the immenseness of that desert.

It now felt as if the trek through The Desert of Transition would stretch the disciple daughter's wearied faith beyond the point of breaking. She was deeply troubled as she questioned whether she would be able to endure the journey across what had become a painfully quiet and dry place. She was also troubled by the silence that had developed between herself and her traveling companion. It wasn't that the Shepherd had left her or that He had made Himself unavailable. He continued to offer Himself in relationship. He was right there in the desert with her. The situation had become more one of simply running out of things to say. She found it sadly ironic that she had the undivided attention of the Master Rabbi and couldn't think of a suitable topic for conversation. For the first time in their relationship she felt intimidated or unsure of herself. She guarded her words as she didn't want to complain or to show a lack of maturity. She also didn't want to disappoint her teacher with silly questions. Her pride had built a wall between them and her fear of disapproval shrugged off the love that was so readily available to her.

The disciple daughter's footsteps grew more labored as she became more deeply entrenched in the desert's sand. The sun's rays seemed more direct and its heat much more intense. This leg of her desert journey was marked by blistering heat and sandstorms that blasted at her skin and burned her throat. All she could focus on was her misery and on reaching this trying journey's end. She was no longer able to enjoy her time in transit with the Son. She was uninspired in His presence and embittered as she could not understand how the Shepherd could let His dear one go through such affliction, heartache and loneliness. Little tears trickled down the disciple daughter's sun burned cheeks as she tried to remember that even now she was being held by the Lord's strong arm and that these trials were of the Father's design. She worried that she would disappoint Him even as she tried to assure herself with His promises to complete His good work within her. She remembered the lavishness of the love that the Father had never failed to pour out in times past. She recalled His mercy and knew that He could do far above anything that she could dare to hope or imagine if she would only continue to submit to His perfect will. Sadly, recounting the Father's blessings and magnanimous character only seemed to make the harsh touch of the desert sands sting even more. The disciple daughter wanted to believe that the Father loved her but right now in this moment she wondered why He did not simply have compassion upon her and bring this journey to an end.

The disciple daughter was plagued with doubt and began to fear that perhaps her Father had uncovered the great sin and multiple flaws that she had buried away even though she had worked so hard to keep them hidden. She worried that His discovery of her shortcomings might have caused the need for extended time in this desert place. She was frightened to think that the accumulation of dross in her life was even greater than God had anticipated and that perhaps He was stalling or delaying His decision to increase her territory because He had determined that she was unfit. It haunted her to think that this was the explanation for the delay of the King's blessing and the probable cause for His allowing her path to become so difficult to travel.

Overwhelmed by insecurity and an awareness of her shortcomings the disciple daughter began to wonder how she would ever make it out of this desert place victoriously. She had lost the full assurance that she once had in the strength of her faith and in the depth of her wisdom. She prayed for grace as she continued to place one foot in front of the other and tried to keep focus on the Father and to trust His character even though she was uncertain of His purpose. The intimacy that she once felt with the Son had grown cold and her communication with the Father was silenced. The disciple daughter realized at one point that she had even stopped singing praises as she painstakingly stretched her stride to place her feet within the footsteps that the Shepherd had measured out in the sand ahead of her. She continued on in obedience but had lost all joy for her journey.

The Wanderer's Prayer

Lord, I need your presence-
Your calming Spirit,
Your soothing voice,
Your reassuring touch.
I need to hear the beating of your heart
and to see the tears of compassion welling in your eyes.
Above all Lord, I need to know that victory is mine
And that you are moving me forward.

Give me a hope, a vision and your assurance today as I wait on you.
Amen.

Meandering

Scripture Meditation

"It takes eleven days to go from Horeb to Kadesh Barnea by the Mount Seir road."(Deuteronomy 1:2).

"The Children of Israel had moved about in the desert forty years until all the men who were of military age when they left Egypt had died since they had not obeyed The Lord."(Joshua 5:6).

Musing

Bible scholars estimate that the Children of Israel took roughly forty years to complete what should have been a two week journey. We can read the repeated accounts of these wanderers in the book of Exodus and of their constant murmuring, grumbling and complaining as they traveled toward their promised land. They attacked their leadership. They blasphemed their God. Whenever the journey got the least bit uncomfortable they begged to go back to Egypt and to return to their lives of captivity (Numbers 14:2-4).

How could it have taken those stubborn Israelites forty years to travel a distance that could have reasonably been covered in eleven or twelve days? It would not be far-fetched to speculate that there must have been a great deal of *meandering* or of wandering about aimlessly in circles without clear direction or a straight path. Joshua 5:6, listed in the scripture references above, describes the action of the wandering Hebrew Children by using the phrase *"moved about"* rather than by using a phrase such as "marched directly through" or "set a straight course". *Moved about* seems to suggest a less linear or direct journey and the picture conjured up by the wording would be similar in context to that of the word *meander*.

When an author uses the word *meander* she is usually referring to something that moves lazily and circuitously along a twisted and serpentine path. Cattle meander in green pastures effortlessly chewing on their cud on hot and hazy summer mornings. Children meander down a path from the bus stop toward home at the end of a long day at school. They stop to pick a flower, to climb a fence or to kick a can. They seem in no hurry to arrive at home to begin their homework or to attend to their afternoon chores. Their lingering footsteps have no direction or set pattern or want for clear destination.

A stream meanders along its banks. It bends and roams from beginning to end and twists and turns as it narrows itself against the harsh and rocky environment encountered along the way. The little body of water only widens back up again when the course it follows leads through softer and more welcoming terrain. Such a meandering stream does not seem to wish to expend the necessary force or strength required to cut a straight path through the oppositional rock or to keep its breadth and depth at a constant measure when running into resistance or pressure. Perhaps it has reasoned that it is easier to be flexible or to change one's course when confronted with the giant boulders or solid immovable obstacles that block a more direct pathway. It chooses rather to slowly detour its path and pass without confrontation around the object preventing a more direct route. The caution to that little brook is that if she is left to meander aimlessly within uncharted banks for too long she may eventually double back in intricate and tortuous patterns until she cuts herself off from the life source that started her flow and she ceases to exist altogether. Too soon the aimless passing of time may lead to the passing away of that charming little brook.

The Children of Israel were meant to walk straight through that desert, not to meander aimlessly and hopelessly within it. God purposed their path just as He prepares a path for each of us. He led them out into the wilderness at that exact time in each of their lives for an express reason. Likewise every growing disciple daughter will go through a desert experience designed to be a time of deepening her relationship with her heavenly Father and of clarifying His call on her life (Psalm 4:3, Mark 1:17). The Lord will discipline and refine those whom He loves (Hebrews 12:6). He will use their time in the desert to transform them into a closer reflection of His image (2 Corinthians 3:17-18).

The wilderness was intended as a place of purification and readiness for God's chosen people before they entered into the fulfillment of the covenant promises that He had made to them from the beginning. The time spent there in that wide expanse of unknown terrain was to be a time of spiritual preparation and of strengthening the bonds between these tribes of people, their appointed leaders and their God. Contrary to what their whining and complaining might have suggested; it was never God's intent to leave His chosen people in that wilderness engaged in aimless wandering. He knew what was waiting up head and was there to guide their every step and to meet their every need.

God knew that there would be giants to overcome and rivers to ford before His people would reach their promised destination. He also knew that this rag tag group of Bedouins was going to have to be united and organized under a central point of leadership to victoriously overcome the enemies that still awaited them. He knew that His Children would need to be stripped of the excess weight that they carried out of Egypt if they were going to successfully maneuver their way across that desert. His proud people would also have to be humbled and yielded if they were going to hear what He would speak to them through His appointed leadership.

God gave The Children of Israel a leader, laws to govern their behavior, signs and evidence of His presence, and nourishment for their physical, emotional and spiritual beings. He was their Jehovah-Jireh and as such was readily available to meet their every need. The Children of Israel chose their winding and twisting path of doubt and discontent rather than selecting one of obedience and trust. Theirs should be a cautionary tale to those of us traveling across desert sand today.

It is not the Father's will for any disciple daughter to spend too much time meandering. He is the same God today as He was for the Israelites and as such our appointed desert wandering has an ordained purpose in His plan. Our wandering is meant to have a beginning and an appointed end. Hallelujah! Every daughter of the King can rest assured in the knowledge that our time in the desert is not meant to last forever. Soon dry desert sands will give way to green pastures (Psalm 23).

The God who calls us His own is still Jehovah- Jireh. He will prove Himself available to meet the sojourning disciple daughter's every need. He can and will accomplish all that He purposes in the lives of those who decide to surrender obediently to His good plan rather than to circumvent His will and to complain about His provision. God will use this time apart to remove anything and everyone who is a distraction or a hindrance to His ultimate desire; which is that of ushering His children into their promised inheritance.

Some of us may stubbornly choose to meander far too long murmuring there in the dust and dryness without yielding to the divine purpose for which God brought us to this place. Others will compromise and decide to learn to adjust, to be flexible and to become more tolerant of the desert extremes. That compromise may even lead them to attempt to plant a garden in the sand and to set up housekeeping there among the rocks and boulders. They will simply choose not to expend the faith and the force needed to push through the hardship and to victoriously pass to the other side. These sojourners will determine to settle for less rather than to endure until they reach the Promised Land that is waiting just beyond the desert's borders. They will have forgotten the Father's promise that if we do not grow weary in seeking Him and in following His desired path we will reap the promised harvest in the proper time (Matthew 24:13, Galatians 6:8-10). A small number of those among us will simply give up and sadly die there suffocating in their difficulty and pain. The choice to follow any of the above scenarios will be made by each sojourner and the outcome will be the consequence of each disciple's will.

Dear pilgrim, the choice is ours to either walk directly through the wilderness or to meander too long there. A victorious desert trek will require that we claim our inheritance with faith and hope and discipline ourselves to keep our focus on the Lord and His purposes. We can remember His promises and rely upon the truth of His Word to strengthen us and to carry us as we push forward into the land flowing with milk and honey, riches unfathomable and joy unspeakable. God calls us but leaves the decision to follow and to persevere totally within our control.

Heart's Cry

Lord, teach me to recklessly abandon the minutia and distraction of daily life to seek you and to go out with you in purpose and in faith. Help me to respond in excitement and anticipation when you call to me. Strengthen me to persist through the difficulty and to endure through the trial .I trust you as the Almighty God who is able to do the impossible and to bless beyond measure. Teach me to be still and to know that you are God; to know your voice above all others. Call me back when I meander too far from your paths of righteousness. Do not allow me to cut myself off from your guiding presence. Flow unhindered through me. Amen

Transforming Resistance

Scripture Meditation

"Submit yourself, then, to God. Resist the devil, and he will flee from you. Come near to God and He will come near to you. Wash your hands, you sinners, and purify your hearts, you double-minded. Grieve, mourn and wail. Change your laughter to mourning and your joy to gloom. Humble yourselves before the Lord, and He will lift you up."(James 4:7-11).

Musing

Why are we surprised when we determine to step out in faith and all hell literally breaks loose? Are we not marching into the territory of our enemy? Do we assume that Satan, upon hearing us approaching, will throw open the garden gates to a rosy path and welcome us as we move forward to usurp his authority and claim freedom for his captives? How could we expect anything less than that he would seek to cause us to falter and to fail at each endeavor to overtake him? It is foolish to assume that any enemy of war would lay down his weapons or resign his power easily. Therefore, as we dare to move more deeply into our enemy's territory we should be forewarned that our encounters with him will require greater faith and stronger resistance. We need to remember that our enemy and his minions study us just as we have studied them. Though he is no equal to the captain of the Lord's army; he searches for our weak spots and vulnerabilities and seeks to know our secret thoughts and prayerful planning as we grow in our faith and become greater threats to his devised plans.

As we co-labor together with the Lord, we must remember that resisting the devil and crucifying the flesh is our part of the transformation process (Galatians 2:20, James 4: 7). God will not resist the devil for us any more than he will demand that we submit to His own sovereign authority. Resisting the devil and crucifying our flesh are the obedient transactions of our free will and are our responsibility as co-laborers in the process of our spiritual growth and the "working out of our salvation" (1 Corinthians 3:9, 2 Corinthians 3:18).

Notice in the passage from James chapter 4 listed above that the author starts his dissertation with the call to submit to God before he issues the command to resist the devil. These two transactions of our will are interdependent and support one another in such a way that the more submitted we are to God's sovereign rule and the more we are being led by His Spirit, the easier it becomes for us to identify the tactics of our enemy and to thwart his attempts to trip us up. We cannot resist the devil successfully until we are submitted to God. This is due to the fact that our ability to resist the devil is accomplished through the empowerment of the Holy Spirit within our lives (Ephesians 6:10-13). It is God's power activated and working within us that exposes and defeats our enemy. True resistance does not rely upon personal wisdom or strength (1 John 3:8, Ephesians 6:10). When we humbly submit ourselves to our God by an act of our will we enable the Holy Spirit to overcome the enemy. We are more than conquerors only through Christ Jesus not by our own ability or strength (Zechariah 4:6, Romans 8:11, 35-37). It is the disciple daughter who is surrendered to the life of Christ within her and thus leading a spirit led life that overcomes her sinful nature and slays that old snaggle-toothed lion (Romans 8:1-9, 2 Corinthians 3:17, 2 Peter 5:6-9).

If we are instructed by James to "resist" the devil then what does this action entail? What does it mean for one *to resist* or to *become resistant*? When used as a verb the word "resist" means to exert force in opposition. The laws of physics state that the exerted force would have to be in equal proportion to the oppositional force if it is to stop any forward advancement of that opposing object. Likewise, that resisting force would have to be of greater strength to overcome or to defeat the force that it opposes.

It is interesting that, by definition, something that is resistant does not crack or succumb to pressure. It is not brittle or fragile and can be stretched or compressed under great pressure and then spring back into its original shape when released. We can conclude then that being resistant requires being flexible. Just as the athlete must train and stretch to avoid stiff muscles and ridged necks that could become sore or stressed, the disciple daughter who desires to resist the enemy must train and stretch her faith. Resistant faith must be flexible faith. The disciple who defeats the enemy is the one who can "get bent out of shape" and stretched beyond capacity and still remain pliable in the hands of the Lord. Her faith would not break when submitted to great pressure.

James understood the concept of overcoming faith being flexible faith when he told his readers to submit to the Lord in order to resist the devil (James 4:7). We become more able to resist the enemy and to *push back* against his pressures by becoming more pliable in the hands of the Lord. Power to overcome the enemy is achieved by being strong in the Lord, by trusting His character, and by submitting to His headship. We can resist the pressure to break or to give in to Satan's temptation by standing on the foundation of God's truth and then surrendering up our flesh and our will to that truth (Hebrews 6: 13-15, James 5:7-8). Our faith will shield us but it is the contents of God's Word that puts the enemy on the run. Its truth exposes his lies and his cunning (Hebrews 4:12-14).

Recall that each time Jesus did battle with Satan He did so by claiming the truth of God's Word and then submitting to the authority of God (Matthew 4:1-11, Luke 22:36, 42). He countered all attacks against His character and doubts about His message by using the phrase: "It is written". There was no need to call upon any other authority or legitimization. Jesus recognized that if God had said it then there could be no argument against it. Likewise, the embattled disciple can resist the pressure to break or to give in by standing firm on that which we know is truth and then surrendering the outcome of the battle to it (Hebrews 6: 12-15, James 5:7-8). Circumstances may appear to speak in defiance of God's promises while our emotions may mislead us. We cannot resist our enemy by placing trust in either of these.

Resistant faith is founded upon relationship with God. We become flexible when we can rest in His sovereignty and such rest becomes easier when we know His character. The disciple of the Lord cannot submit to the will of God nor stand upon the truth of His Word if she does not know the content of His character along with the contents of His Word. Resistant faith believes God because it knows God. It communes with God. Flexible faith knows God to be wholly God and recognizes that nothing could be more trustworthy than His character (Hebrews 6:16-18).

The Lord is our Commander in Chief and it is His covenant promises that provide our protection and the authority under which we strike out. Our flesh is made resistant and the enemy's attacks are thwarted only with the truth and authority of God's covenant. We march into the enemy's territory under the banner and the commission of the King of Kings. Submission to His leadership offers protection because when we bow our necks in surrender to His yoke they cannot be broken by another without first penetrating His authority and control over our lives. God's protection can only be extended when we are in right relationship with Him. According to James, resistance is predicated upon submission; and submission requires right relationship. If we are not submitted to the Lord then we are not acting under His leadership or covered by His banners. In short, we are out on the battlefield of our own volition, relying upon our own strength and cannot effectively resist the enemy.

In conclusion, our first responsibility when the enemy comes attacking is to submit to God. There is a required progression and order to our actions. Resistance cannot be activated until we have submitted to allow the wisdom, power and discernment of God to be released. Lunging back against that old lion or going out on the attack before submitting to the will of the Lord is the equivalent of aiming a gun that contains no ammunition. We will be ineffective. Whenever we engage in spiritual warfare we must be submitted to the will of God, listening for His voice and discerning His leading. Our faith is made invincible when it rests on these two immutable facts: Jesus is truth (John 14:6) and God cannot lie (Titus1:2).

Heart's Cry

Father God, I submit to your authority and yield to your Holy Spirit. Empower me now and strengthen my faith that I might resist the onslaught of the enemy. Teach me to discipline my flesh and to hunger and thirst after your truth. Let me submit to your authority as my sovereign king.

Release your wisdom and discernment within me. Give me a desire to read your Word and to study your ways. Establish your precepts and laws in my life that they may govern my steps. I claim my birthright as your daughter and shout victory over my enemies in your name. Amen

A Mighty Fortress is our God

Scripture Meditation

"Whoever dwells in the shelter of the Most High will rest in the shadow of the Almighty. I will say of the Lord, "He is my refuge and my fortress, my God, in whom I trust." Surely he will save you from the fowler's snare and from the deadly pestilence. He will cover you with his feathers, and under his wings you will find refuge; his faithfulness will be your shield and rampart. You will not fear the terror of night, nor the arrow that flies by day, nor the pestilence that stalks in the darkness, nor the plague that destroys at midday. A thousand may fall at your side, ten thousand at your right hand, but it will not come near you. You will only observe with your eyes and see the punishment of the wicked.

If you say, "The Lord is my refuge," and you make the Most High your dwelling, no harm will overtake you, no disaster will come near your tent. For he will command his angels concerning you to guard you in all your ways; they will lift you up in their hands, so that you will not strike your foot against a stone. You will tread on the lion and the cobra; you will trample the great lion and the serpent.

"Because he loves me," says the Lord, "I will rescue him; I will protect him, for he acknowledges my name. He will call on me, and I will answer him; I will be with him in trouble, I will deliver him and honor him. With long life I will satisfy him and show him my salvation." (Psalm 91).

Musing

God promises to be a mighty fortress, a strong tower and a very present help in times for trouble (Psalm 46:1, Psalm 91, Psalm 46:1). A fortress, however, cannot be a place of shelter or protection for those who refuse to enter in. Seeing it off in the distance and then setting up camp just outside its walls does nothing. So it is with us. Our loving heavenly Father is available to us. He promises to provide shelter and to be our sufficiency when we come to Him in our time of need or discouragement but we must decide to take Him up on His offer and to *enter* into His presence. We enter into His protection and He becomes our present help in times of trouble only through our submission, repentance, relinquishing of control and focusing on His Word and His will. Choosing to approach a situation in any other manner will leave us outside of His strong tower and without a promised place of refuge.

Submitting to the Lord and keeping focus on God provides an impenetrable fortress for the disciple. Temptations, tribulations, worries and other worldly concerns cannot disturb her there. That is because all thoughts, imaginations and anxieties must first present themselves to the gatekeeper or the Holy Spirit (2 Corinthians 10:4-6). It is when we cast down our imaginations and bring them bound and captive to the Lord's chambers that we obtain victory and peace in the midst of our circumstance. We are to cast all our cares upon Him resting in the assurance of His great love (1 Peter 5:7). Whatever it is that is preventing you, Disciple Daughter, from entering into the strong tower of the Lord in the midst of your present situation; won't you enter in? The King awaits you there.

"Our God is a God who saves. From the Sovereign Lord comes escape from death."

\- Psalm 68:19-20

Heart's Cry

Father, I long to enter boldly into your chambers and to present my needs to you there. Help me to humble myself and to obediently yield to your will. I want no other besides you. I know that you alone are mighty to save me. Search me now and know me. Forgive my sin and provide me the solace and assurance of your presence. Amen.

Persevering Persistence

Scripture Meditation

"So now Go. I am sending you to Pharaoh to bring my people the Israelites out of Egypt."(Exodus 3:10).

"Therefore, say to the Israelites: "I am the LORD, and I will bring you out from under the yoke of the Egyptians. I will free you from being slaves to them, and I will redeem you with an outstretched arm and with mighty acts of judgment. I will take you as my own people, and I will be your God. Then you will know that I am the Lord your God who brought you out from under the yoke of the Egyptians. And I will bring you to the land I swore with uplifted hand to give to Abraham, Isaac and to Jacob. I will give it to you as a possession. I am the LORD."(Exodus 6:6-8).

"Moses reported this to the Israelites, but they did not listen to him because of their discouragement and cruel bondage."(Exodus 6:9).

"And on that very day the LORD brought the Israelites out of Egypt by their divisions"(Exodus 12:51).

Musing

It would appear, based upon my studies and research on the life and ministry of Moses; which are drawn primarily from the book of Exodus in the Old Testament, that I am not the only one who has questioned whether God was serious when he called me. Examples drawn from Moses' life certainly run parallel to my own experiences and feelings right after I answered a call to ministry and launched out into this walk of faith. Moses met obstacles, questioned God's timing and like most of us, was full of "whys", "how comes" and "whens" even as he stepped out to follow the Lord.

From my perspective it makes perfect sense that a man noted for his great humility would have begged God to send someone else to command Pharaoh to release the Israelites (Numbers 12:3, Exodus4:13). Moses questioned God's choice of him for a voice piece to speak to the demagogue of Egypt; after all, he was never considered eloquent of speech (Exodus 4:10). God's timing wasn't exactly convenient for Moses either. He was settled into his father-in-law's household and had started a family of his own. Packing up his wife and sons and going back to Egypt where he was still remembered as an outlaw criminal probably wouldn't have been his first choice for relocation; but he obeyed.

As Moses obediently stepped out in faith there were a few indisputable facts upon which he could secure his footing. First of all, Moses knew that God had called him (Exodus 3:4-11). He also knew that God was with him (Exodus 3:12). Moses had the full assurance that God was tasking him and equipping him for this particular ministry at this particular time (Exodus 3:14, 4:17). God also provided Moses with physical evidence that He was listening with compassion to each of his objections and to his repeated announcements of obvious shortcomings. Moses soon ran out of excuses as God sent Aaron to him when he said that he didn't like public speaking and responded to each of his objections with a show of His great power and faithfulness. Moses set out on his mission with no question or doubt that he was doing the LORD's will.

Above all, I have learned that the story recorded from Exodus 3:4 through Exodus 12:50 is a story of persevering persistence. When we examine the word *persistence* as it relates to the story of the release of the Hebrew Children from their bondage we must consider the separate acts of persistence motivated by the will of three different individuals: Moses, God and Pharaoh.

First we observe the persistence of Moses as he continued to be obedient and to exercise faith in spite of his insecurities and fear of failure. He returned to Pharaoh again and again despite the increasing severity of the plagues God unleashed upon the land following each refusal on the part of Pharaoh. He also continued to reach out to the Children of Israel and persisted to deliver God's message of hope to them even while dealing with their stubbornness and refusal to listen (Exodus 6:9).

Despite all the evidence of God's calling, provision and faithfulness to Moses, I cannot help but observe that everything did not go off smoothly or without a hitch for the reluctant deliverer. While scholars do not agree on the exact amount of time that lapsed from the point at which Moses returned to Egypt to obey the LORD's commission until the point in which Pharaoh complied with Moses' request and let the Israelites go free; they will agree that it did not happen overnight (Exodus 4:29, Exodus 12:50). The deliverance of the Hebrew Children did not occur without opposition and obstacles and scripture does not report rosy pathways simply because Moses obeyed the call of the Lord and stepped out in faith. God did not accomplish the deliverance of His people instantaneously and the will of God was not achieved without a great stretching of Moses' faith or without his persistent perseverance.

In addition to the persistence of Moses and its impact on this story we should also consider the persistence of Pharaoh; as misguided as it may have been. The ruler persisted in pride and arrogance and refused to humble himself or to submit to the will of the LORD. Rather than yield, Pharaoh tried to compromise with God's demands. Pharaoh considered himself as one likened to a god and arrogantly believed that he was in a position to negotiate with God Almighty- the God above all gods (Exodus 8:25,28,10:11,10:24). He did not wish to be obliged to God by seeking mercy and tried to retain control and to save face even as the plaques increased in intensity and as the toll taken upon his people and his land multiplied (Exodus 8:10). Pharaoh was persistent in his rebellion and each time the pressure let up he returned to his stubbornness and inflated ego.

Finally, we must consider the persistence of God, as this persistence is the most important and effectual influence of the three. Moses persisted and Pharaoh persisted but it was God's persistence that gained freedom from the bondage of Egypt for the Children of Israel. The successful deliverance of God's people was not dependent upon the will of Moses or the desires of Pharaoh but rested completely in the persistent mercy and persevering love of God. God's persistent love for His people combined with His unquenchable desire to keep His covenant promises motivated Him to patiently persevere in His dealings on the behalf of His children (Romans 9:14-18).

From the beginning Moses complained that he was inadequate to make any demand of Pharaoh and suggested that God find someone else to do His will (Exodus 3:11,4:13). He then questioned the LORD's tactics and motivations for allowing greater suffering to befall the Israelites after presenting the initial request to Pharaoh (Exodus 5:22). Later, Moses offered proof that he was not the right man for the job by pointing out the fact that even his countrymen were not taking his pledge of redemption and deliverance seriously (Exodus 6:12). He reminded His creator once more of his faltering lips and slow tongue before approaching Pharaoh for a second go round (Exodus 6:30). Despite Moses' consistent whining and God's anger with his cowardice and insecurity; God persisted and sent Moses back to Pharaoh to demand that Pharaoh let His people go so that they might freely worship Him (Exodus 5:1,7:16,8:1,8:20,9:1,10:3). God persisted in making His demands known to Pharaoh and graciously disclosed the consequences that would result should the stubborn ruler refuse to submit.

God tirelessly listened to Moses complain and whine. He held back His anger and met each of Moses' objections with a solution (Exodus 4:14). He armed Moses with his brother and everything else that he would need to fulfill the mission that God had commissioned. God persisted to move in grace toward Moses despite Moses' undeserving actions. God could have acquiesced and then chose another more suitable, less whiney deliverer to take Moses' place but He persistently continued His work of deliverance in and through Moses. It was God's persistent grace that transformed Moses into the deliverer who was able to take the Children of Israel beyond the boundaries of Pharaoh's kingdom and across that wilderness in which they came to wander.

The loving heavenly Father also persisted in grace toward those hard-headed Israelites who refused to believe that He had sent Moses to them (Exodus 4:5,6:6-9). The Hebrew children had come to know lives that were filled with despair and focused on bondage. They would not believe or trust in the love of God or hold fast to the promises that He had made to their forefathers. God graciously looked beyond their grief-stricken fear and lack of faith and responded to the cries of His people (Exodus 6:7). He persisted to fulfill the covenant promises that He made to their forefathers despite their lack of faith (Exodus 6:8). Their God persevered and proved Himself faithful to His unbelieving people and almighty to His unrelinquishing enemies (Romans 9:16).

Jehovah persisted. God Almighty continued in His work on behalf of His people. He persisted against the hardened heart and inflated ego of Pharaoh. He persisted against Moses' cries of insecurity and inability. The God of Abraham, Isaac and Jacob persisted until those doubting Israelites saw the deliverance of their LORD and watched the angel of death pass over their households while striking the homes of the Egyptians (Exodus 12:24-30).The God above all gods persisted until the self- proclaimed demagogue of Egypt bowed to His authority and asked for a blessing from the humble leader that Yahweh Himself had sent (Exodus 12:32). God used Pharaoh's rebellion to prove His mighty power (Romans 9:17). He persevered in His sovereignty and persisted in His mercy and His grace. Jehovah- Jireh persisted until those Egyptians gladly tucked gifts of silver and gold as well as extra clothing into the belongings of their now freed slaves as they hurried them on their departure. God's persistence set His people free after four hundred and thirty (430) years of slavery (Exodus 12:33-36,40). God persistently persevered until He had accomplished all that He had desired and foreordained.

The good news that we can take away from the story of The Exodus is that God Almighty persists in the same manner as He did then within our life circumstances today. He will graciously persist against all of our whining and insecurity. He will persist against our sinful rebellion and arrogant pride. God will persist against the lack of belief found in those in need of deliverance and He will persevere against all the rulers of principalities and powers standing in defiance of His will. The King of Kings will persevere as He overturns His enemy's kingdoms and delivers Satan's stolen riches as spoils into the hands of His people. Our heavenly Father will never fail to prove Himself faithful and almighty. He will accomplish all that He foreordained for us and all that He wills for our lives (Jeremiah 29:10-12). If this God be for us then who can persevere against us (Romans 8:31)?

Heart's Cry

Almighty God, King of kings and LORD of Lords, teach me to persist in believing in your persistence. Help me to remember your faithfulness and your great love when I appear to be up against a power that will not bow or an obstacle that will not move. Let me know your presence and trust that you are working on the behalf of your people even when I do not see your hand or understand your acts. Father, do not grow weary with my complaining and my lack of faith. Be persistent in your grace and mercy toward me. Persist also in your faithfulness toward those whom I love who are in bondage and captivity. Bring their deliverance. Amen

Recognizing the Lord's Authority

Scripture Meditation

"He got up, rebuked the wind and said to the waves: "Quiet! Be Still!" Then the wind died down and it was completely calm. He said to his disciples, "Why are you so afraid? Do you still have no faith?" They were terrified and asked each other, "Who is this? Even the wind and the waves obey him!"(Mark 4:39-41).

"Night and day among the tombs and in the hills he would cry out and cut himself with stones. When he saw Jesus from a distance, he ran and fell on his knees in front of him. He shouted at the top of his voice, "What do you want with me, Jesus, Son of the Most High God? Swear to God that you won't torture me!" For Jesus had said to him, "Come out of this man, you evil spirit!"(Mark 5: 5-8).

"For this people's heart has become calloused; they hardly hear with their ears, and they have closed their eyes. Otherwise they might see with their eyes, hear with their ears, understand with their hearts and turn and I would heal them"(Matthew 13:15,Isaiah 6:9-10).

Musing

It is difficult to understand how the disciples who traveled with Jesus, who sat under His teaching and witnessed His miracles, were suddenly terrified when He exercised His authority to quiet the storm that was sweeping over them (Mark 4:39-41). These doubting disciples had engaged in intimate daily contact with Him (Mark 4:30). They had heard Jesus' parables and teachings on faith just a few hours before this storm began to brew. Surely if they had been listening at all then His presence should have been enough to quiet them during this sudden gale. Rather than exercise faith and rest in His love, they trembled with fear in His presence.

These men did not yet recognize or comprehend the full authority of Jesus. If they had then they would not have been fearful watching the Master sleep in the very same boat that they occupied. Seeing His peace and His composure should have caused them to be at peace as well, but instead they were filled with doubt and concern for their well-being (Mark 4:38). It is ironic that He had spoken with them earlier about the rapid growth of a mustard seed and yet their faith was still so small.

Now they shook in terror as they whispered among themselves and questioned who this man who walked among them might really be. Their intimate knowledge of Jesus should have caused them to abide peacefully in God's presence in the midst of the storm. Instead they were just trying to hang on with clenched teeth and white knuckles until the turbulence was over. They heard His teaching. They touched His flesh. They saw His miracles; but they still did not understand that this carpenter's son was the omnipotent Son of God. If they had understood then their experience in that storm tossed boat would have been quite different.

The disciples didn't recognize Jesus as the Son of God but the waves did. The minute Jesus rebuked the wind and spoke to the waves they both died down and things got completely still (Mark 4:39). All of nature is filled with signs of His awesome power and extolls His holy name (Psalm 19:1-6). Creation is maintained by His authority and operates under His dictates (Colossians 1:16-17). Those waves recalled His hand and recognized the voice that now commanded them as the one that spoke them into existence (John 1:1-14). How sad that it took creation's acknowledgement of Jesus' authority for His disciples to realize that Jesus was far greater than they had conceptualized. If they had known His authority and had acknowledged His omnipotence they would not have been rebuked by Jesus for being cowardly in His presence (Mark 4:40-41). They limited their Master and fell victim to fear as a result.

The story continues with the disciples failing for a second time to recognize the full authority of their Master. This second scenario occurred upon their arrival on dry land after Jesus subdued the storm. It was there that Jesus' followers encountered a demon possessed man calling out from among the tombs. His disciples may not have recognized Jesus' authority but those demons waiting on the shore certainly did. The legion of demons that inhabited the tormented man cried out to Jesus even when they saw Him from a great distance (Mark 5:6). That huge demonic legion bowed itself at Jesus' feet and those evil spirits begged Him repeatedly not to torture them but to let them be (Mark 5:6-11). They knew who He was and called Him: *"Jesus, Son of the Most High God"* (Mark 5:7).They knew their fate was in His hands and had to beg His permission to leave their host and to enter a herd of pigs (Mark 5:9-13).

The people from the nearby towns who witnessed Jesus' interaction with the demonic man also recognized His authority. It was their acknowledgement of who He was that left them unsettled. When the neighbors of this man who had been so tormented saw that he was now healed, delivered, dressed and sitting calmly in his right mind they became afraid and pleaded with Jesus to leave their region (Mark 5:15-17). They didn't ask Him to stay with them or to deliver and heal more folks from their community. They feared this authority that accomplished what they had been powerless to do for so long. They feared this love that had brought life back to a man who had been left in the tombs without hope (Mark 5:3-5). They feared what they did not understand and as a result they wanted Jesus gone from among them.

How is it that the men who traveled with Jesus and were closer to Him than His natural earthly family did not fully understand the secrets of the Kingdom of God that He shared with them? How could they see Jesus every day and not recognize that He was God incarnate? How could they fail to see what the heavens declared and the demons feared? Perhaps the disciples' eyes were blinded to the authority of the one who walked among them because they had stopped looking at Jesus in awe and had stopped expecting greater things of Him. Perhaps Jesus had become too familiar and they had grown satisfied with the status-quo. Perhaps, as Scripture foretells, they had grown calloused and even with the very Son of God in their presence they did not believe that Messiah had come and was sleeping in their boat (Isaiah 6:9-10).

The Lord is as equally present and active in and around our circumstances and our everyday lives as He was in the lives of those who walked with Him while He was physically dwelling upon the earth. Yet we do not always see Him and recognize the power of His full authority in our unexpected and challenging circumstances. Often, all that is lacking in our ability to see Him and to recognize His authority and power over a situation is for us to shift our focus. God is always present and longs for us to recognize both His sovereignty and His goodness in our daily lives. Our Father also wants us to learn to rest in that sovereignty and goodness. Learning to pay attention to His presence and to remain at peace under His authority will mean the difference between victory and defeat in storms and other trying circumstances of life.

Heart's Cry

Oh Father, give me ears to hear the rustle of your garments and closeness enough to know your presence in my daily living. Show me your face. Give me greater understanding. Turn to me and give attention to my cry as I reach out to you in total faith and dependence. Give me the faith to believe in your authority with the same measure that your enemies believe in your authority. Grant me discernment enough to recognize your presence as they recognize your presence. Amen

Walking in Our Authority

Scripture Meditation

"For this people's heart has become calloused; they hardly hear with their ears, and they have closed their eyes. Otherwise they might see with their eyes, hear with their ears, understand with their hearts and turn and I would heal them"(Matthew 13:15,Isaiah 6:9-10).

"But you will receive power when the Holy Spirit comes on you; and you will be my witnesses in Jerusalem, and in all Judea and Samaria, and to the ends of the earth."(Acts 1:8).

"The Spirit of the Lord is on me, because he has anointed me to preach good news to the poor. He has sent me to proclaim freedom for the prisoners and recovery of sight for the blind, to release the oppressed, to proclaim the year of the Lord's favor."(Luke 4:18-19).

"For in him we live and move and have our being. As some of your own poets have said, "We are his offspring."(Acts 17:28).

Musing

Unlike the disciples traveling with Jesus who were caught in the unexpected storm that rose up, Isaiah saw the Lord; in full authority, high and exalted and seated on His throne (Mark 4,Isaiah 6:1). Isaiah heard the voices of the heavenly host as they shook the doorposts and thresholds singing God's praises (Isaiah 6:4). He also heard the voice of the Lord when God commissioned him. Isaiah recognized the Lord's authority over his life and responded to Him in humble obedience (Isaiah 6:8).

Could it be that Isaiah saw and heard what those fear stricken disciples failed to recognize simply because he was listening with opened ears and looking with spiritual eyes? Did Isaiah see the Lord seated on that throne simply because he was looking for Him and seeing Him there was exactly what he expected to see? Whatever the reason for the disciples' failure to recognize the authority of their leader it cost them dearly. Those men were unable to recognize the authority of Jesus and as a result unable to apply that authority in the circumstances of their lives. Conversely, Isaiah saw the Lord, recognized His authority, repented and submitted to His call. The Lord God honored the devotion of Isaiah, cleansed him from his sin and appointed him as His prophet (Isaiah 6:6-13). From that day forward Isaiah's life would never be the same.

What will be most important to the success of our mission as ambassadors of God's kingdom is that we recognize the authority with which we come and that we learn to exercise that authority in our lives and let that authority change our daily walk. We need to recognize that the one who had the right to all authority and power; Jesus Christ, has now bequeathed His authority and power to us. God has given Christ's authority to us because of Christ's work on the cross and His victory over sin and death.

Christ has called us and has sent us out to share the gospel (Matthew 28:18-20). He has given us authority to drive out demons, to heal the sick and to set the enemy's captives free (Mark 3:13-14, Luke 4:18-19). We must recognize our authority and be certain that we walk in it because our enemy recognizes the authority of Christ within us, even as we approach from far away. He will seek to stop us and to impede the work of the gospel. He will seek to uproot every seed that we sow before it has time to take root (Matthew 13:18-19). We do not need to fear the enemy, however, despite his best efforts; if we are walking in the authority of the one who sent us.

Christians have been incorrectly led to believe that we are fighting a foe whose power is superior to ours and possibly even equal to that of God. This teaching is not biblically correct. The authority of God, which backs every believer who comes in His name, is a power infinitely greater than that which backs God's enemies (1 John 4:4, Romans 8:37). All the powers and principalities in heaven and earth are compelled to recognize our God's sovereignty (Ephesians 6:11-18). We can rebuke Satan with our God-given authority and he will bow when we call out the name of Jesus, the Son of the Most High God (Philippians 2:10).That name is the name above all names and it will subdue our enemy and accomplish what human remedies could not do and human reasoning cannot fathom (Acts 4:12).

Disciple Daughters, we must remember to be listening if we would hear and watching if we would see. We must seek if we are to find answers and knock if the door is going to be opened to us. After recognizing God's sovereign presence, we must search out the contents of His Word to find His truth and to speak and move with His authority (Acts 17:28). We must also wait on Him in prayer to receive specific instructions for our lives. We must be waiting in expectation if we are to receive anything from the Lord. Imagine what could be accomplished for the kingdom if each of us would simply claim our authority, and like Isaiah, respond to the Lord's commissioning in obedience. Imagine the things that could be accomplished in the life of the disciple daughter who dared to keep believing in the unlimited authority of God rather than to surrender to fear and doubt (Mark 5:32-36). Imagine what changes will occur in our lives and our walks when we open them up to the authority of God.

Heart's Cry

Open my eyes Lord and allow me to see Jesus. Help me to walk in the authority of my birthright that Christ reclaimed for me through His redemptive work on the cross. Teach me to trust your sovereignty and to dwell in your presence in peace even as the storm rages. Give me victory over the enemy's deceptive tactics and lies as I stand in the authority of your Word. Amen

Scoffers, Scorners and Unbelief

Scripture Meditation

"He sighed deeply and said, "Why does this generation ask for a miraculous sign? I tell you the truth; no sign will be given to it. Then He left them, got in his boat and crossed to the other side."(Mark 8:12-13).

"But they mocked God's messengers, despised his words and scoffed at his prophets until the wrath of the LORD was aroused against his people and there was no remedy."(2 Chronicles 36:16).

"Whoever corrects a mocker invites insult; whoever rebukes a wicked man incurs abuse." (Proverbs 9:7).

"And God said," I will be with you. And this will be the sign to you that it is I who have sent you... God said to Moses, "I Am Who I Am." This is what you are to say to the Israelites: "I Am has sent me to you."(Exodus 3:12,14).

Musing

The ministry of the disciple of Christ is to model redemption and to lift up Jesus. Jesus said that if *He* be lifted up *He* would draw all men unto Himself (John 12:32). Followers of Christ are to walk in close relationship with the Lord and to seek to represent Him in all of their daily interactions with others. The closer a disciple becomes to the Lord, the more she will begin to reflect His likeness just as the closer one stands to a mirror the clearer and sharper the image reflected back becomes. In the process of walking in relationship with Christ we cannot help but be changed and will begin to reflect His character to those around us. They will then have the opportunity to either accept or to reject the truth of who He is.

The presence and indwelling of the Holy Spirit within the life of the disciple will force those around her to acknowledge that life force and to then make a decision regarding what position, if any, they will give Jesus within their own life. Some people we encounter will be made uncomfortable with this call to make a decision. Members of our audience may respond to the evidenced life of Jesus in their presence with mocking, anger, ridicule or contempt. They may react to the convicting presence of the Holy Spirit with fear or rebellion. Some of those whom we encounter may ask us to prove what we know to be true and perhaps offer up sarcasm and criticism for our beliefs and of our walk. Others may be prompted by the Holy Spirit and sense a stirring within their souls but respond to this gentle nudge with doubt and confusion. They may walk away with unanswered questions and refuse to allow time for their spiritual muddle to settle or for the Holy Spirit to provide the clarity they seek.

Whatever someone's response may be to our walk and our witness, we must remember that it is God's work to change people and the Holy Spirit's job to convict. The disciple is simply to speak of what she knows to be true and to testify of God's work in her life. We must make every effort to be gentle in dealing with those whom the Lord places in our path and consciously choose to respond to them in His grace. We must present His truth without resentment, bitterness, or anger. Ambassadors must also be careful not to be drawn into quarrels, speculations or vain arguments. We can avoid each of these pitfalls by praying that the Lord will lead all people to repentance, and recognize that it is His work to demolish all strongholds and to expose the lies of the enemy that hold people captive (2 Timothy 2:24-25,2 Corinthians 10:4-6).

Each encounter that a disciple has with a scoffer, or with those who scorn the testimony of the Lord, provides an opportunity to either reflect our Father's image or to surrender to a reaction that is being prompted by our own flesh. We can choose to discipline our flesh and to submit our emotions or we can choose to "play war" and to seek validation or vindication and retaliation. Seeking to be an instrument of God's grace and reconciliation will require that we make a conscious decision to be gracious and to maintain our composure. If we desire for God's spirit to be evident within us and for His grace to pour through us then we must surrender our right to be right and our desire to be vindicated. This will not be an easy task but Jesus has promised to provide us His peace to stay us in trying and difficult situations. We must decide when in the midst of those circumstances whether we will accept His promised peace and exercise the fruits of the Spirit to govern our fleshly nature (John 14:27, Galatians 5: 22-25). We must remember that we allow the enemy a foothold and possibly quench the working of the Holy Spirit whenever our flesh rises up in anger, bitterness or contentious pride. Likewise, choosing to love, to forgive and to walk in humility with those who revile and criticize us prevents the enemy from undoing all that God seeks to accomplish (Ephesians 4:17-30). The later will only be possible when we recognize who we are in Christ Jesus and who it is who has sent us (Exodus 3:11-14). Having our identity is securely anchored in Christ releases us from the fear of condemnation, ridicule and rejection; because we know that we are fully loved and wholly accepted (1 John 4:9-12). Then it will be God's unconditional love and Christ's grace toward us that will compel us to be gracious and loving towards others.

Scripture offers repeated warnings against entering into vain arguments with hard-hearted mockers. Such behavior accomplishes nothing for the kingdom of God; and as pointed out above, may often be counterproductive. Jesus did not waste time providing proof of His authority to the deceitful Pharisees or others who mocked Him or sought to entrap Him with religious debate. He measured His words carefully and then left their presence altogether when He had finished speaking (Mark 8:12-13). In one incidence recorded in Scripture, Jesus distanced Himself from any further argument or entrapment by putting an entire lake between Himself and those who sought to entangle Him. He saw no point in wasting more of His time and breath by trying to validate His point. Jesus knew that His Father would deal with these folks and therefore had no need for vindication or to justify His position. His identity rested securely with His Father and not in the approval or acceptance of man.

When the Lord sends His disciples out He will allow the grist mills of difficult experiences to grind them into feed corn for His sheep. The most trying of confrontations can be used to accomplish greater refinement in the life of the disciple who is yielded to God's will and seeking to display

His character (John 16:33, John 17:23-25, Philippians 2:13). Living a life that is totally surrendered to God's call requires a conscious awareness of His presence and of His active involvement in each situation (Exodus 3:12). It requires trusting that responding with the Holy Spirit's discernment and yielding to God's sovereign wisdom will sustain our peace and develop patient longsuffering for others within us. Exercising such faith will allow us to present those whom we encounter to the Father and to relinquish all our control over them. Doing so will then enable the Lord to work His will and to meet their needs unhindered by our interference and fleshly desires (Philippians 4:19, Hebrews 4:16).

The spiritual authority of the disciple becomes obvious to others in direct proportion to her willingness to submit to God and to trust the matter to His hands. It is when we are submitted to God's sovereign will and operate motivated by His unconditional love for others that His divine character can be evidenced and His transformative grace be exemplified. When we allow the Holy Spirit to live in us and humbly yield our bodies, hearts, and souls for His service, Jesus is lifted up and Christ is victorious. Living this way causes even our enemies to be at peace with us and makes those who oppose Christ His footstool (Proverbs 16:7, Hebrews 10:13).

Heart's Cry

Lord, I ask that when my spirit is embittered or when I become exasperated with others that you would guide me by your counsel and remind me that you are always with me and holding me in your right hand. Help me to firmly place my identity in you and to remember that you have written my name in your palm. I am yours. Set a watch on my mouth, Father, that my words may be pleasing and honorable to you. Strengthen my heart and purify it. Keep my eyes fixed on you and help me avoid the snares and traps of the wicked by walking in humble obedience with you. Amen

A Father's Correction

Scripture Meditation

"I am the true vine, and my Father is the gardener. He cuts off every branch in me that bears no fruit, while every branch that does bear fruit he prunes so that it will be even more fruitful."(John 15:1-2).

"He will sit as a refiner and purifier of silver; he will purify the Levites and refine them like gold and silver. Then the Lord will have men who will bring offerings in righteousness and the offerings of Judah and Jerusalem will be acceptable to the Lord, as in days gone by, as in former years."(Malachi 3:3+4)

"My son, do not make light of the Lord's discipline, and do not lose heart when He rebukes you, because the Lord disciplines those he loves, and He punishes everyone He accepts as a son. Endure hardship as discipline; God is treating you as sons."(Hebrews 12:5-7).

"But He knows the way that I take; when He has tested me, I will come forth as gold."(Job 23:10).

"No discipline seems pleasant at the time, but painful. Later on, it produces a harvest of righteousness and peace for those who have been trained by it."(Hebrews 12:11).

Musing

In our times of testing and correction, whether our path is steep and rocky, dry and barren or muddy and full of pitfalls, we must remember that all of life is not an uphill climb or a sojourn through a lonely desert. There is a time for struggle and for weeping but those moments will soon be followed by a time for the sampling of wine and for jubilee and celebration. For every vine there is a season for rest, for growth, for harvest and for wine and joy. Pruning is only one aspect of the work of the gardener or the keeper of the vineyard. Take heart in knowing that the vine is only pruned at precisely the right time, in the right season and in the exact measure that will guarantee future growth and development. The vineyard master studies his fields and knows the age and the condition of each and every vine. He knows precisely when and how to prune each vine to produce the greatest and sweetest possible yield.

Pruning and correction are not always the disciple's set of circumstances. The Lord will not always deal with us in this manner. When we are struggling in the desert heat or enduring the rocky terrain of the mountain climb we must recall the green pastures and babbling brooks of refreshment that our Shepherd also lovingly provides. We must keep perspective to avoid becoming resentful or bitter toward our Father's correction and reproof. All things work together to accomplish the Father's sovereign purpose in the life of His beloved when we are yielded to His will (Romans 8:28). His sovereign purpose is to bless us and not to harm us (Jeremiah 29:11).

Refining is an exacting and precise process that is carried out in stages and over time. The silver is not always located in the middle of the melting pot or centered within the most intense heat. It is not continuously exposed to the strictest of testing. The silversmith carefully watches as he calculates the time consuming process of purification. He holds that precious metal cautiously and lovingly in the middle of the hot blue flames because he has an investment in the outcome of the process. That silver is his purchase and his investment. He bought it and he owns it. The silversmith knows that the finished product will bear his mark and carry his name. It will speak of his creative ability.

An experienced lapidary artist never leaves his silver to face the flames alone but patiently and cautiously watches every passing moment. The goal of this painstaking process is not to destroy the metal but rather to bring forth what the jeweler knows is hidden deep within. Thus he must be certain that the metal is not scorched or destroyed by spending too much time within the intense heat. He will regulate the intensity of the fire to encourage the burning off of dross but will not allow the flames to destroy his precious metal's total composition. Likewise, the watchful silversmith will be careful not to allow the silver to rest too often or to cool too soon. He will stop the process of firing and refining only when he sees his face reflected within the silver that he has purchased and has so lovingly labored over.

Each sojourner who makes the decision to follow Christ will endure hardship; Scripture is very clear on that point. Trials and testing each play a contributing part in the process of our transformation as we are working out our salvation. While no one looks forward to the difficulties of life with joyful anticipation; we can rest assured in knowing that this season of testing, of pruning and of refining has a greater purpose in our lives. The Lord disciplines those whom He loves. He does so because He has an investment in the outcome. Our Father is removing the dross and painstakingly laboring over us so that we might reflect His character and glorify His name. We bear His image and are the purchase of His blood (Revelation 5:9-10). It is not His desire to destroy us nor to cripple us; but rather to make us sons and daughters who are wholly acceptable and who can worship Him in righteousness (Malachi 3:3-4,Romans 12:1-2).

Scripture tells us that the gardener uses pruning shears to enable the vine to bring forth more fruit (John 15:2). It also tells us that submitting to the discipline of the Lord, as unpleasant as it may seem, will bring forth a harvest of righteousness and peace (Hebrews 12:11). The Lord knows the path that we take (Job 23:10). As our sovereign Shepherd, He places us in the way of trial and tribulation with purpose. He leads us through the valley of the shadow of death with intent (Psalm 23: 4). As our silversmith, He lovingly watches and controls the heat of the flames to which we are exposed and He never leaves us (1 Corinthians 10:13,Hebrews 13:5). He doesn't just sit idly by while we endure. Our Lord is the fourth man in the fire, right beside us and lovingly watching our keep (Daniel 3:25). When we have come through this time of trial and of testing and correction all the world will see our Father's face emblazoned on our being and we will be jewels in His crown that bring glory and honor to His name (2 Corinthians 3:18).

Cinthia W. Pratt

Heart's Cry

Father, even as I go through this time of testing and of refining help me to secure my faith in the truth of your Word as I call your promises out to my flesh, to my enemy and to my Father who hears me. I surrender myself to your loving correction and submit my will to yours. Fill me with your words, your thoughts and your Spirit as you lead me forward and make my pathway straight. Search me, try me, know me and reprove me. Bring me out of your refiner's fire in newness of life and in victory for your glory and to your praise. Allow me to walk on holy ground before you and to worship you in transparency within your holy throne room. Amen

A Life-changing Relationship

Scripture Meditation

"When they had finished eating, Jesus said to Simon Peter "Simon, son of John, do you truly love me more than these?"(John 21:15).

"See, I am doing a new thing! Now it springs up; do you not perceive it? I am making a way in the desert and streams in the wasteland."(Isaiah 43:19).

"Greater love has no one than this, that he lay down his life for his friends."(John 15:13).

"I tell you the truth, unless a kernel of wheat falls to the ground and dies, it remains only a single seed. But if it dies, it produces many seeds. "(John 12:24).

Musing

It could have been that Jesus asked His impetuous follower, Peter, if he loved Him again and again that day for the benefit of all those gathered on the beach and within earshot of Peter's response. Perhaps He wanted to be certain that everyone witnessed Peter's commitment. It is equally possible that Jesus repeated His query simply because He wanted to be certain that all those standing near the campfire recognized the importance and the value of what He was now asking. Perhaps Jesus knew that hard-headed Peter had to be asked more than once to assure that he gleaned the full meaning of Jesus' questioning. Whatever His reasoning, Jesus asked Peter multiple times in that single conversation if he loved Him more than anyone or anything else (John 21:15).

Each of the three times that Jesus asked Peter if he loved Him above all else he followed up with a command to feed His flocks. Jesus was seeking to convey to Peter that if he loved the Lord he would take it upon himself to care for Jesus' followers as a shepherd would care for his sheep. This must have been a strange conversation for Peter as Peter was a fisherman; he was not someone who tended sheep. Peter knew fish. He understood nets and tides and casting out into the deep to bring in a catch. He knew nothing of tending sheep. He did not know how to lead or how to feed livestock. Yet when Jesus spoke to Peter about proving his love for the Lord he did not use examples drawn from Peter's profession and from the patterns of his old life. He wasn't asking Peter to use his natural abilities nor was He asking him to go back to doing what he knew best. Jesus was now calling Peter to dare to do something unfamiliar and new; something totally outside his training, his natural affinity and his comfort. Jesus was asking the fisherman to feed and care for His flocks on His behalf.

Fish were easy. They were caught to be eaten. They did not require constant protection against predators or to be warned of impending dangers such as sudden storms of shifts in the tide. Fish did not have to be supervised, rounded up or directed in their comings and goings. They did not look to the fisherman for daily nourishment or require his touch for the healing of their wounds. Fish did not need to trust a fisherman. They had no need for knowing his voice. Fish were Peter's livelihood. Catching them provided him with an income and filled his stomach. Peter went to the deep where they swam when he needed something from them. He cast his nets and there they were.

Identifying with Jesus that day on the beach meant that Peter's life was about to change dramatically. Gone were the early morning hours spent in solitude on the lake. Peter was about to be the leader of a flock and be surrounded by others that he would need to feed, to supervise and to safely lead. Jesus' sheep were now going to look up to Peter and to depend upon him.

Accepting this call to be a shepherd over the Lord's flocks would require new skills and new ways of thinking and of expression. Peter, the shepherd, could not rely upon his own natural capability, training or resourcefulness to get his new job done. Peter was also going to have to change his disposition as he could not respond to sheep in the same manner in which he interacted with fish or with other fisherman. He was going to have to lead these folks forward into a lifestyle that was first exemplified by the Good Shepherd who was no longer physically available to teach or to guide His flocks. Jesus had resurrected and was leaving this earth when He entrusted the care of His flocks to Peter.

Jesus was asking Peter, the fisherman, to surrender his nets and to remain on the shore. Peter the evangelist, the fisher of men, was now being called to be Peter the pastor, Peter the mentor, and Peter the friend. Peter was called by Jesus to touch and to calm, to love and to lead as he had seen Jesus touch, love and lead. The Good Shepherd was leaving the care of His flocks to someone else; someone that He trusted and in whom He had poured out Himself during His time here on earth. Peter was now going to have to consider the welfare of others and to focus on interacting, leading and sustaining the lives of those whom God had entrusted to his care.

Peter may have felt useless and of little value in matters related to sheep. He was gruff with worn hands, leathered skin and a reactive spirit. He was impetuous and his behavior was often dictated by his emotions. He was known to speak and to act without thinking. These were not the characteristics that one would seek in a leader nor were they attributes in which sheep would find comfort or solace. Jesus knew however that this gruff fisherman was equipped to be a loving shepherd because it was He who had equipped him. Jesus knew Peter. He had spent time traveling dusty roads from town to town with this fisherman and Peter had proven his willingness to go where the Lord guided. (Matthew 4:19). Jesus also recalled how this man of the seas had no fear even as he jumped from his boat into the water to walk to Jesus on the waves (Matthew 14:22-23). This fisherman was fully equipped to lead the Lord's flocks even if he did not yet realize it.

The Lord had full confidence in Peter because He knew what He had taught him as Peter sat with Him in the still of the night and learned at His feet. Jesus also saw how Peter had grown and softened during their time together. Jesus looked beyond the exterior of this fisherman and knew his heart. He knew his faith and his great love for others. He would not have entrusted the care of His beloved sheep to Peter otherwise.

It is often at precisely the time when we perceive ourselves of little value and at the point of being our most useless that our life is opened up for God to enter in and to act in miraculous ways. He can and will do a new thing in us and through us just as He did in Peter. All He asks is that we surrender our bodies and our being to His service. God can do the impossible and extraordinary in each of us. He can take us places we have never been and use us in ways that we would have never dared to even imagine if we are willing to leave all that we know and to extend ourselves beyond our comfort and natural capability.

Being used in life changing ways requires letting of our own expectations and feelings of inadequacy as we surrender in love to the Lord. It also requires resting in the assurance of who we are in Christ Jesus when doubts and insecurities plague us. We can step out in faith to do things beyond our natural affinities and talents by trusting that the God who is calling us is also equipping us. He is shaping us to do something new empowered by His strength and guided by His Spirit. It is when we submit and allow the Lord to do all that He desires that He is able to transform us into the instrument of His choosing and the vessel of His blessing. Greater works can be accomplished in us when we are willing to be cleansed of our hardness, insensitivity and impatience and to be softened through the indwelling presence of the Holy Spirit.

Take comfort, adventurous disciple, in knowing that every follower of Christ is fully equipped with all that is needed to accomplish what Christ is calling her to do. The intimate knowledge of her savior and the contents of God's Word provide His wisdom and His discernment to guide her. She carries the mantle of God's authority and is fully empowered through His Holy Spirit. The Good Shepherd is the bread of life and the living water that she will carry to those who are spiritually hungry and in thirst and her loving heavenly Father will provide all that she requires to feed and to care for those whom He entrusts to her leadership and care.

It is interesting to note that when Peter jumped from the boat this last time he had to swim to the shore. He did not walk on the waves to meet with the Lord in the water as he done before. Once the fisherman arrived on dry land he found the risen Jesus asking him to leave all that he knew, and to let go of all that he relied , upon to dare to do what no fisherman before him had done. Jesus asked a rugged fisherman to now be the loving shepherd of His flocks. The Lord is making the same request of each of us. He is asking us to forsake all that we know to live a life that is just as unexplainable and just as impossible. Will we dare to see beyond the sphere of human possibility and limitations to walk into the impossible, incredible, miraculous blessing of our divine calling? How much do we love the Lord? How much do we love His people? May we, as His disciple daughters, learn more and more to focus on ourselves less and less as we offer up our lives as broken bread and scattered feed corn for the Good Shepherd's flocks.

Heart's Cry

Lord, I lift my life up to you. Take it now and do extraordinary things that I cannot imagine both in me and through me. Move my thoughts far above the realm of finite thinking to think beyond human possibility. Remind me that nothing is impossible with you. Increase the territory that you have entrusted to me. Mold me, transform me, change me and shape me into the vessel that you desire me to be. Empower and equip me through the power of the Holy Spirit to do even greater works than those who walked with you before me. Amen

Pondering God's Timing

Scripture Meditation

"Be still, and know that I am God: I will be exalted among the nations, I will be exalted in the earth."(Psalm 46:10).

"For my thoughts are not your thoughts, neither are your ways my ways," declares the Lord. As the heavens are higher than the earth, so are my ways higher than your ways and my thoughts than your thoughts."(Isaiah 55:8-9).

"I am the Alpha and the Omega, the First and the Last, the Beginning and the end."(Revelation 22:13).

"Woe to him who quarrels with his maker, to him who is but a potsherd among the potsherds on the ground."(Isaiah 45:9a).

Musing

God is eternal and dwells within the spiritual realms. He is not bound by the ticking of the clock nor does He measure His actions in increments of time. Our Father is never late neither is He ever early. It is impossible for Him to be either as He alone is sovereign and eternal. He set time in motion and established the routines and patterns of all life. The Great I AM is and was and ever more shall be (Exodus 3:14+15). He is always on time because He holds and controls all time (Colossians 1:17). Knowing these things should keep His trusting disciple at peace while waiting for the things that are yet unseen, and for the plans that are yet unknown, to come into fruition and to appear. Our Father's planning and timing is better than our own because He is the source of all wisdom and knowledge (Proverbs 2:6,Romans 11:33-36,Colossians 2:2). Waiting disciples can trust the timing of the Father because only He knows the precise moment when He should enter our situation and accomplish His glorious purposes. Remembering that He alone is the sovereign God that spoke all things into existence should enable us to trust His love and to surrender our thoughts to His wisdom even when His promises are delayed (Exodus 33:18, James 1:5).

In times of solitude and of shadow, God's beloved can be at peace by opening up our spiritual eyes and trusting all time to our Sovereign's keeping. It is when we are content to be shut up with Him and can become unconcerned about the passing of time that God will show us the secret things that He holds in His hands and in His heart. Because He can speak of things that are not as if they are and call things into being that do not yet exist, our Father is able to move beyond our limited understanding to give us a greater vision of His glory and a clearer understanding of His character (Romans 4:16-17). His spirit will carry us as we are lifted beyond the veil to see as the eternal Father sees. The Lord's abiding presence is the guarantee of His promises. He is the presently and always available sufficiency for every dry and expectant soul who is waiting for His outpouring (Joel 2:28-32).

God has a purpose for the empty spaces in our experience as well as for their duration. Our resting and waiting for the Lord must not be equated with sitting idly by. Our waiting is with purpose and by design. God has a plan for the times of isolation and quiet. He has a purpose in His delays. Submitting our lives to His sovereignty requires acknowledging that God often chooses to move in ways that are not like those of our choosing and that do not coincide with our plans. As our sovereign, God will move when and as He chooses. While it is true that nothing and no one can thwart His good plan; it is also true that the Creator can only accomplish His complete and perfect will in the lives of those who wholeheartedly wait in anticipation and expect Him to come in. It is then that He will fill those empty spaces and quiet times with His presence and His purpose. In times of solitude and patient endurance we must trust that our maker has not forgotten us and that He is at work within us as well as on our behalf.

There will be times in our lives as disciples when everything appears closed to us and nothing is moving. At other times the Lord will impart a vision to us of something that has not yet materialized in the physical. Our only option in such situations will be to be still and to trust that God is moving even though

He seems to be distant or silent. We must believe that His words will come true at their proper time and wait though it appears that He has forgotten us or is not coming (Luke 1:20). We must learn to find rest in God alone and to place all of our expectations at His feet (Psalm 62:5-6).

Often we are not supposed to comprehend but rather simply to have childlike faith and to trust in our Father as a child in arms would trust. As His dearly beloved children we can wait with no worry and we can rest with no fear because we know that He holds our tomorrow secured in His great love. We can be still until He opens up a clear path and wait patiently until He breaks through the obstacles that presently block your progress. Our Father knows the path that we take and, because He does, we can follow His lead. We can move only when He says to move and be confidently still when He is still.

The Lord's sheep are never frantic, never panicked, and never at a point of desperation. They are not frightened when He seems silent. They have learned to trust the immutability of His promise and to secure themselves in the knowledge of their maker's holy character.

Heart's Cry

Oh Lord, Teach me the fine balance of knowing when to wait and when to step out in faith though my path seems unclear. When you reveal something to my spirit that has not yet materialized in this world teach me to faithfully wait for its birth and accomplishment. When I am frightened and insecure teach me to commit my ways to you and to rest in the knowledge of your holiness. When you are silent, help me remember that silence does not mean absence. Father, give me the childlike faith to wait secured in the knowledge that you love me and that you know what is best for me. Let me find peace in the assurance that you alone know when your plans for me should and will be accomplished. Amen

The Wide Wilderness of Want

The disciple daughter had no idea that surrender to the Father's refining would lead her into such a dry and lonely, unwelcoming place as that Desert of Transition had proven to be. The intense heat of the desert sun's direct rays had left the pilgrim parched and dry. She was noticeably tired and weary as she began to sense the sand slowly giving way to harder, denser ground under her feet. Though the desolate territory over which she had crossed had proven challenging for the King's daughter; she was happy to report that she had grown in those difficult times and was thrilled to now be coming out victorious. It was true that at several points in her desert trek she could not help but question what she had done to cause such a trying set of circumstances. She remembered how those at home had sometimes passed judgment upon other travelers who had recounted stories similar to her desert predicament. They had questioned how a disciple with a proper relationship with the Father could find themselves alone in the desert without a church home or the company of friends and family to share their journey. These folks suggested that it was unconfessed sin and rebellion that had caused the harsh surroundings of such travelers. The disciple daughter now knew from personal experience that these judgments were untrue and refused to allow condemnation of others to hinder her continued transit. She smiled with encouragement as she realized that the Father had been at work all along. It was the Father who had prompted her to leave home and who had faithfully guided her pilgrimage across those desert sands. He had ordered her steps and ordained her path. The wearied pilgrim had found the Lord to be her fountain of life even through the most dry and difficult desert sands. Just as the Father had promised, when she completely yielded her will and focused on the footsteps of the Shepherd she received His divine joy to add to her own and began to feel the peace of His presence. Her countenance actually began to glow as the dross of her flesh was painstakingly removed from within her. The disciple daughter knew that she was a closer refection of her Father as she stepped out of that intense desert heat. She now had full confidence that her Father would provide all that she needed even in the harshest of environments and driest of deserts. She learned that the Shepherd's company was indeed enough to satisfy even her deepest thirsts and that when she sought Him she found Him. He was true to His word and never left her or forsook her.

As the wearied pilgrim stepped up onto firmer and higher ground she found that her faith was quietly reassured and her level of encouragement was somewhat elevated. She smiled a smile of satisfaction and was proud of what she had accomplished in her journey across those desert sands. She also smiled to know that her desert time was over.

The disciple had completed the first phase of her journey and was now ready to rest and to receive the inheritance that the Lord had promised. She peered into the horizon just beyond the treetops and longingly surveyed the open skies for any sign of the King's banners flying overhead. She knew that seeing such banners would indicate that the Father was in residence within His dwelling place. Now she hoped to see those magnificent colors unfurled ahead in the distance. She let go a heavy sigh when she could not yet see them but felt certain that if she simply took a few more steps forward she would see those flags hoisted just above His towers and gloriously waving her home.

The sun burned and wearied traveler had expressed an air of relief when the hot sands were finally gone beneath her feet. Sadly, her relief was quickly stifled as she scrambled up the nearest hill to survey the new terrain opened up before her. She was happy to be out of the desert, but did not recognize this new and strange place that ran right along the border of the desert sands. From her newly gained vantage point she could see what appeared to be absolute vertical terrain on the outer edge of this wilderness in which she had just entered. Although the air did seem much cooler than that of the desert, this place was a dark and tangled expanse filled with thorny underbrush, tall hedges and twisted trees. She pulled her cloak more tightly around her shoulders as she left her perch to venture more deeply into this newly entered territory. The damp chill suddenly sent a shiver up her spine. The air grew thick and wet and the sky was darkening overhead. The sun that the traveler had grown so accustomed to seeing high in the desert sky was suddenly blocked from her vision. She could no longer feel its warmth and wondered if it could be possible that this new territory would be marked with an even greater sense of loneliness and social isolation than what she had experienced crossing those hot desert sands. She tried to remove those oppressive thoughts from her mind but felt physically heavy as the light of her spirit was suddenly overshadowed by an awareness of her personal insecurities and feelings of awkwardness. The disciple knew that she did not wish to remain in this land of shadows any longer than absolutely necessary and began to search for the quickest route out of this wide wilderness of want.

The horizon was etched with the outline of the surrounding borders of mountains. They cast tall shadows on the ground below and appeared as if they shot straight up and rose for more than a mile into the sky. The disciple daughter sighed as she was already dreading what might lie ahead. The thoughts of having to climb those seemingly perpendicular cliff sheers before entering into her promised territory left her in despair. She had set out on a journey that she felt certain was orchestrated by her loving Father only to now feel as if He had once more abandoned her. The reassurance and encouragement that she felt just a short time ago now dwindled. The disheartened disciple grew angry as she compared the overwhelming difficulties of her journey to the seemingly easier paths required of those back home who seemed content to remain right where they were. It seemed unjust that her desire to answer the Lord's call would be met with such obstacles. She left her perch and the disconcerting view of the mountains that loomed ahead to return to the thicket of brush through which she must now maneuver.

One of the disciple's greatest joys had been sharing encouragement and fellowship with others. Making her way through this wilderness left her feeling so totally alone. She had hoped that when she completed crossing the desert that her journey's solitude would be over. She did not know if she was prepared to travel another leg without companions and the interaction of others to encourage her steps. Judging from the dense vegetation and narrowness of the paths the disciple was now facing, it was obvious that caravans of merchants did not travel these hiking paths. She laughed at the absurdity of heavy laden camels bearing merchant's wares trying to maneuver through these winding and rocky trails. She could barely squeeze her way through some of the narrow passages snarled with branches and thorns. The traveler found that she could carry very few of her personal belongings into this wilderness and stopped long enough to empty her pack of all that was unnecessary to her survival. She had let go of the few treasured belongings that she had carried from home as well as the souvenirs that she collected to remember her trek across the desert. The pilgrim traveler was resentful to discover that she was now traveling through a wilderness of want and despair rather than enjoying a time of contentment or of resting in the fulfillment of promises believed and dreams hoped. She also discovered that even though she had left her home with a planned route in hand, that plan no longer fit the pattern that her travels were taking. It was as if the map that she carried with her was for some territory other than the one in which she now sojourned. Nothing made sense and her journey with the Shepherd was not as she had planned.

Squeezing through these narrow and rocky wilderness trails soon proved extremely exhausting and difficult. The trails were littered with debris and there were dense patches of heavy vegetation and huge rocks and boulders jutting out from amid downed trees. A great number of tree branches had been broken with wind and weather. These had fallen but were prevented from totally reaching the ground by the dense expanse of canopy overhead. There they now hung casting shadows and cutting off any light that were originating from the sky above. The small lamp that the Shepherd had provided would now be the only source to light His follower's path. She had to keep the oil well full and carry the lamp close to her heart if she was to prevent the casting of shadows directly across her path. The reduction of depth perception that occurs in such shadowed lighting offered another impairment to the disciple daughter's eyesight. Her greatly distorted vision would cause rocks and roots to appear closer to the ground or smaller than they actually were. The disciple daughter had to be extremely careful and use a discerning eye as she made her way; if not, her footing could appear deceptively easy and moving too quickly could cause her to stumble or fall. As she moved cautiously forward, she was certain that she would experience many stubbed toes and bruised ankles crossing through this territory of shadowed vision. The disciple learned quickly that she could not trust her own eyes but had to diligently listen for the Shepherd's voice. She had to rely upon her capability to hear Him and trust His leading to guide her safely forward. The disciple daughter reached up to securely tighten the chin strap of her helmet of salvation into place. She knew full well that if one of those branches caught up in the canopy broke free it could deliver a heavy blow to her neck and head.

The disheartened pilgrim's feelings of encouragement and accomplishment were short lived in the face of such spiritual near-sightedness. The desert's refinement had been draining and as the wilderness grew thicker and darker she was certain that any remaining passion and joy would soon leave her. She was cold and weary as she continued praying and calling out to her Father. The disciple daughter continued to earnestly seek His face with each forward step she took into this cavernous wilderness but could not see Him due to the shadows. Though she strained her ears to listen she could not recognize the sounds of His movement in the tree branches just ahead in the distance. The disgruntled daughter of the king soon incorrectly judged her Father as lacking in compassion and slow to respond to her pleas.

The shadows of this land played tricks on the disciple daughter's short sightedness and kept her from realizing that the Shepherd was on the path just ahead calling out her name. He beckoned to His beleaguered follower and asked for a continued willingness to trust Him as they journeyed more deeply into this wilderness composed of the secret passions of her heart, the hidden thoughts of her mind and truest longings of her soul. She followed but was devoid of contentment and struggling to find hope as she brushed branches back from her face and squinted her eyes together in an attempt to squeeze out all available light from the sky. Sadly, she wondered if Christ was in fact her true sufficiency. She mentally went over a list of the items that she had removed from her backpack and worried that she might need them and secretly regretted having left them behind. The disciple daughter worried whether her Beloved would prove to be the greatest fulfillment of her soul and feared that her secret passions would continue to overshadow her view of Him. It was highly conceivable to the disciple daughter, as she traveled through this wilderness of shadows, that her secret desires might trip her up and cause her to forsake her call to follow the Lord. She prayed that Jesus would prove to be her heart's desire and the source of all that she needed. She prayed that her faith could survive this place of soul searching. The pain of her doubt had no sooner entered the weary disciple's mind when her empty stomach began to growl and her thirst cried out to be satisfied. She allowed her mind to wander back to the sweetness of home as the hunger of her wanton soul continued to gnaw at her discontented soul. She secretly longed to be satisfied with things that the Father wasn't quite ready to entrust to her keeping.

A few of the folks back home had applauded the disciple as she discussed setting out on her great adventure with the Lord. Some even praised her as a mighty woman of faith, but now she realized that the truest illustration of her would be that of a rebellious little lamb bleating out a cacophony of cries against dreams postponed, faiths derailed, and hope that was withering quickly. Her emotions overwhelmed her as she felt abandoned, angry and denied by the Father. She was wearied by the stress of transition and longed for the comforts of home. The adventurer wasn't sure if she would ever arrive at a new destination and this land of shadows had made it more difficult to envision where or what her intended inheritance would be. The Father may have called her out of the camp to come away with Him but now all she wanted to do was to go back home, take off her shoes and rest on her laurels. She wanted to laugh and to fellowship with the others she had left down in the valley. She wanted to enjoy the sweet reward of her faithfulness. Her guide promised that the adventure would get better but she secretly longed to go back, if but for a moment, to reclaim those things that she had left behind. The longer the disciple daughter wandered through this twisted wilderness composed of circuitous trails and disappearing pathways the smaller her faith in the Lord and her confidence in His promises became. At one point, the disciple daughter wondered if she would have enough oil to sustain the light she desperately needed to safely traverse through this land of shadows. She had not packed any in her bags and was totally dependent upon the Shepherd to provide more when she needed it. Her ration of bread was greatly depleted as well. She wondered where the Shepherd would find more rations in this wide wilderness that sprawled out before her. She prayed that promises delayed would not become promises denied.

The Shepherd's Leading and Correction

Scripture Meditation

"He maketh me to lie down in Green pastures..." (Psalm 23:2).

"Remember not the sins of my youth and my rebellious ways, according to your love remember me for you are good, O Lord."(Psalm 25:7).

"You have made known to me the path of life; you will fill me with joy in your presence, with eternal pleasures at your right hand."(Psalm 16:11).

Musing

Many times I have chuckled to myself while reading the well-known and beloved passage contained in the twenty-third Psalm that is often referred to as the "Shepherd's Psalm". It is not my intention to be disrespectful; and the words of the familiar Scripture are certainly not in and of themselves humorous. It is my own personal interpretation and life application of these verses that causes me to laugh. For example, the line in verse two that reads: *He maketh me to lie down in green pastures* "conjures up an image in my mind of a rebellious little sheep bucking under the hand of the loving shepherd who is trying to sternly and yet gingerly press that little one down into the safety of the pasture's grass. The shepherd knows that the little one under His care needs rest. He knows that she needs sleep and time for her body to heal and to recover from the day's wanderings. He alone knows tomorrow's journey and the perils of the path ahead. But I can just see that little lamb bucking and bleating and struggling to jump to her feet. She will have none of her shepherd's desire for stillness.

How often have we, as Christ's followers, become worn out and spent little lambs simply because we would not listen for the Shepherd's voice, or heed His warning to be still and to rest before trudging along without sure direction or footing? Tired and weary and often consumed by tears and heavy emotions, we return to the Lord to pitifully plead for energy to complete what we have taken on without His instruction or call to do so. Perhaps if we had just surrendered to His touch and followed His leading to be still we would not find ourselves in our current situation.

I confess that often times I have run headlong into my own self-propelled busyness in an attempt to prove my worthiness or value to the Lord's service. My issue was not in trusting God but in fearing that God did not trust me; that He did not want me, or that somehow He did not consider me worthy of His work. My interpretation of His call to be still was one that led to insecurity and fear of rejection and it was this fear that was prompting me to move, to find something to do, to look busy for the Father. I had allowed my desire to be greater and my fear of being small to override my assurance that I was God's daughter and that He was my *Abba Father* (Romans 8:13-17). If I had fixed my focus on the truth of His perfect love, I would have been more secure in my rest from work, more trusting of His call to refreshment, and better able to cast out this fear that now had me aimlessly expending my energy.

At other times, my refusal to lie down and to be still before the Lord was the result of my fear that if I stood still and were open before Him then He might see something in me that displeased Him. I did not trust the words spoken by the psalmist of a comforting rod nor Jesus' own reminder that He is the Good Shepherd who lays down His life for His sheep (Psalm 23:4, John 10:11). I knew my secret sins full well and was just waiting for God to catch up with me to expose and punish them. I reasoned that if I kept moving and kept busy then perhaps He would overlook my flaws on account of my deeds, or that somehow moving would prevent me from being vulnerable and exposed to His grooming and correction. My logic was that it is far more difficult to fix a scrutinizing and focused gaze on a moving target. I feared the Lord's reproof and instruction and failed to recognize that my Father approached me as His beloved daughter and disciplined me out of His great love and concern for my growth and benefit (Hebrews 12:5-11).

Other times of rebellious refusal to be still before the Lord were prompted by my desire for control and were the result of my stiff neck and arrogant pride. I refused to acknowledge God as my sovereign and to surrender my path to His leading. As a result, when I determined that I had been still long enough, I would devise my own plans and label them as of the Lord. I would then ask Him to bless my efforts after the fact. I wanted my will and to choose my own direction and failed to recognize that no sheep can have two shepherds. Often this little lamb learned too late that if I deliberately wandered away from the Good Shepherd's hedges of protection then He could not rescue me from the calamity of the path carved out by my disobedience. This headstrong sheep misunderstood that the Father's hedge of protection was established to preserve me. I saw hedges and fences as a hindrance to my desire to frolic and to run free (Job 3:23). I placed my life in peril by breaking union with the Good Shepherd and was often dragged away into sin by playing god for myself (Zechariah 11,James 1:13-14). My sinful rebellion blinded me to the truth that the Good Shepherd is the only rightful shepherd. Only He has the God given authority to command His sheep (John 10:14-18). The right to the governance of my life belongs to my creator alone.

Won't you lie down little one? The sheep of Christ's flocks can rest securely in the pastures that He has provided for them. If we will but obediently lie down and bask in the Lord's presence and rest in our appointed times of stillness then He will draw close to us and give our weary souls the gentle whispers of assurance that we so desperately need.

Be still disciple daughter. Allow your Master to work in you and in the path that lies ahead of you. Drink deeply from the quiet waters that He has provided (Psalm 23:2b). Allow yourself to cast off your cares and frustrations to enter into His covenant rest. Be immersed into His springs of living water and drink His peace into every pore. Be totally saturated, consumed, covered and refreshed within His presence. It is there that you will find fullness of joy and great pleasures (Psalm 16:11). Trust His leading and listen for His voice. Yield to the authority of your Shepherd and receive newness of life from your Father.

Heart's Cry

Precious Shepherd, I surrender to your sovereignty over my life. I trust your timing and relinquish my desires to your will. Help me to rest in your presence and to joy in the absence of toil and work. As I wait here help me to demolish the arguments of fleshly doubt and fear that prompt me to run. Remind me of your steadfast love for me. Search me and know me. Be my Shepherd and lead me in your paths of righteousness. Amen

Apart

Scripture Meditation

"The Lord God said, "It is not good for the man to be alone. I will make a helper suitable for him."(Genesis 2:18).

"But if we walk in the light, as He is in the light, we have fellowship with one another."(1 John 1:7a)

"As the deer pants for streams of water, so my soul pants for you, Oh God. My soul thirsts for God, for the living God. Where can I go and meet with God? " (Psalm 42:1)

"This day I call heaven and earth as witnesses against you that I have set before you life and death, blessings and curses. Now choose life, so that you and your children may live." (Deuteronomy 30:19).

Musing

It was God's intended purpose from His creation of the first humans that we fellowship with Him and with each other. He created human beings to be in fellowship and to a contributing part of something greater than ourselves. According to the creation account recorded in the book of Genesis, after God had given Adam life, He noted that it was "not good" that His precious human creation be alone (Genesis 2:18-20). God then created a life-long companion and help-meet for Adam to love and with whom to share his life there in that garden paradise. It would thus appear that God appointed fellowship between humans as His solution for the "not good" condition of being alone.

Humans are communal. We all long to belong and to have the company of good friends. We thrive in the giving of ourselves and the sharing our ideas, thoughts and gifts with one other. Psychologists would agree that a sense of belonging and of being loved is among the most basic necessities to a happy and healthy human experience. Every human being desires to love and to be loved and functions best within an environment that provides the security of feeling needed and of value or importance.

Traveling in the company of good friends makes our path brighter and our journey much more interesting. Scripture teaches us that the counsel of good friends is encouraging and that their words can be both faith building and correcting. Friends can sweeten one another's countenance and help to shave off the rough edges of each other's disposition (Proverbs 27:17). Yet, as we journey through life we will find that our relationships with others will shift and change, move and grow. There will be periods of belonging followed by periods of being on the outside looking in. Interactions with others will offer a sense of connectedness at some times and a feeling of isolation or distance at others. Our life journey may lead us along wide paths with throngs of happy companions followed by narrow paths of solitude and quiet introspection. Spiritual maturity will require that we be content whether fellowshipping in a crowd or traveling in a place of stark isolation.

Many of us recall the bitter sting of not having our artwork chosen to be put on display by an elementary school teacher. We may have been picked last for volleyball, passed over for the cheering squad or uninvited on the shopping trip or to the party. We may have been denied a raise, ridiculed for our appearance, trapped in a loveless marriage, or fear remaining single and lonely despite our desire for a life companion. We become wise when we understand that rejection and isolation each play a part in the experience of being human. Not everyone is going to understand or accept us and we are not always going to be welcomed with open arms into every social situation. Scripture reminds us that Christ came unto His own and that His own didn't welcome Him or receive Him (John 1:11). Our Lord was rejected and despised (Isaiah 53:3). We would be remiss to anticipate that our life here on earth would be any different than His; particularly given that He warned us that this temporal world would hate us (Mark 13:9-13).

Each scenario that life presents requires that the individual involved process and interpret the interaction and then arrive at a conclusion regarding the events that have taken place. It is that individual's conclusions regarding the situation that will then influence her choice for subsequent reactions or behavioral responses. The reaction that follows our interactions, along with our emotional responses to those interactions, will vary according to the system or the "mind" with which we choose to filter and to define the input of the situation. In any given situation, every disciple daughter has the choice to interpret and to respond utilizing her emotional self, her intellectual self, her ego driven self, or her spiritual self (*the mind of Christ*). Each of us freely chooses which of these *selves* we will allow to dictate our reactions and responses to the behaviors of others. We can avoid responding inappropriately only when we chose to respond utilizing our spiritual self or by accessing the mind of Christ and the fruits of the Spirit. Choosing to respond with any of our other selves may cause us to be tempted to feel rejected, abandoned, wrapped in self-pity, unjustly treated, or somehow undesired or *less than*. These feelings may lead to a desire for retaliation, vindication, and a host of other ungodly or sinful reactions. It is only when we choose to operate in our spiritual self, and recognize that these times of emotional stretching have been purposed by our Father for our spiritual growth and refinement, that we reflect an overcoming attitude and gain the victory.

Our attitude can be the same as that of Christ Jesus when we remember that each of these trying encounters does have purpose in God's ultimate plan for our life. It is in these times of self-doubt, social awkwardness or feelings of inadequacy and isolation that God draws us close to Himself. If we will submit to His touch and allow His refinement and reproof then He can increase our courage, strengthen our faith, tear down our idols of need for approval, break off our fear of rejection, and deepen our knowledge of Him. These times can offer us opportunity to prove our God as all sufficient, ever-present, unconditionally loving and ever faithful. Giving our stretching situations over to the Lord's control and allowing His Spirit to speak to us while in the midst of the difficulty enables us to filter our understanding of the events utilizing the mind of Christ rather than reacting with the impulses of our other "selves".

Our heavenly Father loves each and every fearfully wonderful one of us. He desires for us to know Him in His fullness and to value our relationship with Him above all others. He will devise times in our lives to reproof us, to draw us closer to Him, and to deepen our intimacy with Him. In His jealous love for us, God will remove anyone and anything that distracts our attention to Him, impedes our dependency upon Him or quenches our desire for Him. It is only our creator and sustainer who can satisfy the hunger and thirst deep within each disciple daughter. For what each human being desires at their very core is to know their Creator and to be truly known by Him in return (Deuteronomy 4:29-31).

Imagine how Mary felt as she heard the voice of her risen Savior calling her name. She thought that she was alone in that garden filled with death, grief and tears (John 20:1-18). Not only was Mary alone but her interpretation of the scenario also left her feeling lonely and abandoned. Her desires for the companionship of her Lord were left unfulfilled and her inability to comprehend why someone would have stolen Him away depleted her of all joy and hope. Only bitter grief remained as she searched that garden for the answers to the questions that perplexed her soul. Mary chose to react to her situation with emotion rather than with faith.

How sweetly the voice of Jesus must have resonated in her ears as Mary realized that she was not alone and that her Lord was living and calling out to her. If the grieving Mary had continued to be overwhelmed by her grief and blinded by her own despair and pain she might never have heard the sweet voice of Jesus calling to her. Likewise, what secrets did Jesus share with Mary, the sister of Martha, because she chose to quietly sit at His feet and to hang on His every word (Luke 10:38-42)? What joys did Martha forfeit because she was busily going about life consumed with the needs and the opinions of others along with the reputation of her household? Martha would never have the opportunity to go back and to recapture the moments she missed by refusing to sit at Jesus' feet when He asked (Luke 10:41). Each of these three women chose where to focus their attention while in the midst of daily living. Each also chose which "self" they would employ to interpret their situation and influence their responses. It was the chosen response of each different woman that brought about the outcome of their situation.

Heart's Cry

Father, remind me that when I walk with you I am never truly alone. Though others may forsake me you are always available and welcoming towards me. Teach me to sincerely desire intimacy with you above all other relationships, status or things; to hunger and to thirst after you alone and to know you as my sufficiency. Tear down the idols of need for approval, for affirmation or for praise. Teach me how to be content when alone, quiet and still and to value those times as an opportunity to draw close to you. Show me how to sit at your feet and let me seek my soul's fulfillment from you. Thank you for staying near me and for offering me the opportunity to share the secrets things of heaven as I sit at your feet. Amen.

A Season of Patience

Scripture Meditation

"I will stand at my watch and station myself on the ramparts: I will look to see what He will say to me, and what answer I am to give to this complaint."(Habakkuk 2:1).

"There is a time for everything, and a season for every activity under heaven... What does the worker gain from his toil...I know that there is nothing better for me than to be happy and do good while they live... I know that everything that God does will endure forever: nothing can be added to it and nothing taken from it."(Ecclesiastes 3:1-14).

"Be Patient, then, my brothers, until the Lord's coming. See how the farmer waits for the land to yield its valuable crop and how patient he is for the autumn and spring rains. You too, be patient and stand firm, because the Lord's coming is near."(James 5:7-9).

Musing

Patience is not a virtue that is easily found among people living in a society marked by microwave ovens, fast food, and drive through windows that are readily available for everything from banking to pharmacy service. Living in the land of affluence does not contribute to the development of patience or to the acceptance of deferred pleasure. Our lives are transacted within a society filled with all manner of instant gratification, and as such, it is not the natural tendency of our self-centered, want-driven, desire-seeking, sinful flesh to be denied or to postpone the fulfillment of our wants. We live in the land of instant potatoes, instant weight loss, instant credit and cash in advance. Our success driven culture causes us to rush around, to multi-function, to hurry things up and to speed things along. We want things done more quickly and if possible immediately. We move through accelerated education, collect advanced college credit and buy groceries through an automated, self-check-out line. We eat in our cars, text and chat at the dinner table (which is often substituted for a tray in front of the television), three-way call and either record our television shows or order them "on demand" to watch at our convenience rather than wait of a regularly scheduled broadcast time. We don't seem to know how to wait for things to take their natural course and even schedule the birth and delivery time of our unborn children for the optimum convenience of all involved. It would appear that we have forgotten that there is a natural rhythm to life and that everything under the sun has a season composed of a natural beginning and a subsequent ending.

Crops take time to grow, weather occurs in seasons, the sun rises and the moon sets. All things are set into motion by a God who is a God of order (1 Corinthians 14:33,Ecclesiastes 3:1-14). God created the world and all that it contains in a sensible fashion with a perfect rhythm and a natural ordering for the appearance of each item as he created it (Genesis 1:1-2:1). Likewise, He orders our steps and establishes the days of our lives following His design, precepts and laws (Job 14:5,Psalms 119:73-80). Our Creator has a plan and a purpose of each step that we take and when we commit our ways to His wisdom and trust Him with the circumstances of the day it is God who establishes our steps and makes our way clear (Proverbs 3:5-6,Jeremiah 29:11-13).

So then, why do we rush the timing of God's plan and working in our lives? What is the motivation behind our impatient demeanor with our loving Father? Do we believe that we know better than God? What makes us think that we can order our lives with greater efficiency than He who orders and sustains the universe? Can our finite minds comprehend the reasoning and planning of the infinite and omniscient creator? Would any of us dare to presume to take control of His universe and assume responsibility for the well -being of all its contents and inhabitants? How far reaching is the extent of our sinful pride? Biblical history reminds us of a time when the Creator did authorize mankind's dominion over His creation and the result of our sinful disobedience cursed us and all that God had created (Genesis 1:28,Genesis 3:14-16).

True submission in patient obedience does not place fleshly conditions or time constraints on the work of the Lord. Worrying, fretting, growing impatient and then manipulating or plotting an alternate plan is not obedience. Such behaviors will not accomplish anything godly in our lives; as a matter of fact, quite the opposite is true. Choosing to engage in such actions may actually bring disastrous consequences (Luke 12:22-31). Doubt cannot abide in the presence of faith; neither can impatience (James 1:6-8). This is because true patience is rooted in and sustained by faith while impatience is born of pride and doubt. Patience is an act of our will that is predicated upon our faith. We prove our spiritual maturity when we are tested or stretched by our level of patience. Anyone who truly believes that God is sovereign will rest patiently in this knowledge an trust His wisdom. Mature faith will conquer doubt and cause us to be at peace even when we don't fully understand the timing or the motivation of what God is doing. Those who are truly walking with the Lord and experiencing the peace of abiding in His presence will demonstrate such by the gentleness and calmness of their reactions. (Philippians 4:6-7). Faith does not produce fretting or frantic and frenzied behavior. Faith produces peace.

Mature faith trusts the character of God even when unsure of His actions. Logic dictates that if only God knows the future and if He has dominion over everything; then we are wise to submit to His sovereignty and to recognize that only God can change our present situation. Because our God is all knowing, He will do that thing that we ask of Him only when it is the best possible time to do so (Ecclesiastes 8:5-8,Hebrews 2:10). The sad truth is that often we forfeit God's optimum blessing and prevent His perfect will from being transacted in our life because we impatiently take matters into our own hands or fail to trust God's provided timing. (James 1:13-18). We manipulate and maneuver ourselves right out of God's greatest blessing and grandest provision. When we are tempted to become impatient we must slow down, control our impulses and learn to discern the leading of the Holy Spirit. Choosing to focus on the faithfulness of the Lord and submitting to His sovereignty rather than giving in to the impatient desires of our flesh will keep us from sin and temptation (James 1:19-21,Galatians 5:16-25). When we sincerely recognize that God is sovereign over everything and that it is in His hands alone to grant every good and perfect blessing in our lives then it becomes easier to be patient with even the most trying aspects of our lives and to trust the timing of God's plan.

⚜ ⚜ ⚜

Heart's Cry

Father, slow me down to walk in perfect unison with you. Let me wait patiently while you establish my path and prepare the territory that you have preordained for me. Teach me to walk with you, beside you, contented to move one step at a time. Teach me the discipline of patience and strengthen my faith today. I ask that the fruit of your spirit be actualized in my life and that I might walk in a manner that pleases you even when I am stretched and tired. Amen

Contentment in the Journey

Scripture Meditation

"Though the fig tree does not bud and there are no grapes on the vines, though the olive crop fails and the fields produce no food though there are no sheep in the pen and no cattle in the stalls, YET I will rejoice in the Lord, I will be joyful in God my Savior."(Habakkuk 3:17+18).

"I am not saying this because I am in need, for I have learned to be content whatever the circumstances. I know what it is to be in need, and I know what it is to have plenty. I have learned the secret of being content in any and every situation, whether well fed or hungry, whether living in plenty or in want, I can do everything through Him who gives me strength."(Philippians 4:11-13).

Musing

As we progress in our journey here on earth, we discover that our life is lived out in phases and that our journey transpires as we are being transformed from the person who we once were when we were first delivered from the bondage of our former self. We are growing and changing as we are walking into the full inheritance of our promised eternal life in the presence of God. Each of these various phases seems to have its own cadence and pace as we pass through it. Sometimes we run with great vigor and stamina while at other times it seems we can barely crawl. We stop and we start. We rest and we replenish. We sleep and we wake and most of the time we are able to find a sensibility to the rhythm of the path upon which we are traveling.

There are also times when even the most earnest of disciples will wander off course or meander away from a clearly marked and direct path. In these times our journey feels as though we are passengers on a sailing vessel that has launched from the harbor but now is without wind to fill its sails and to allow it to continue on its course. We are at a dead halt in the deep; silent and still, waiting to catch the breath of hope that will navigate us safely to shore. There is no movement, no wind upon which to set our sails. There isn't even a gentle breeze to sooth us as we wait. It is in such times as these that we must learn to be content while we wait for God to work beyond our vision within the unseen realms. We must trust that He will fulfill that which He promised and know that God is always faithful to accomplish all that He plans. We must learn to rest in contentment while our sovereign sets all things in order and activates His plan though His working is beyond our vision and understanding.

There are other times in our life's journey where our path becomes rugged and rocky and our climb is harsh and steep. We find ourselves stumbling among the rocks and languishing in the heat of the dry places rather than frolicking down in the soft meadows filled with pleasant flowers and refreshing streams. We may also discover that there is little in the way of nourishment in these harsh terrains or that there is very little vegetation that is pleasing to our palate. Perhaps what does grow where we are now traveling is bitter or unsatisfying because it is planted within soil deplete of nutrients. We fear that our Shepherd has left us alone without sustenance or refreshment.

Paul stated that he had learned to be content in *whatever* conditions he found himself (Philippians 4:11-13). In Philippians 4:12, the apostle echoes the sentiments expressed by the prophet Habakkuk when he declared that he would praise God whether he was well-fed or hungry (Habakkuk 3). Paul shared that he had learned the secret to living a life of contentment even as he was held prisoner in a dungeon and dealing with ever failing eyesight. That secret is derived from "the one who gives him strength" (Philippians 4:13).

Living a life marked with contentment will require that we recognize Christ as the source of our contentment, as Paul did, because the ability to remain content in difficult circumstances must originate from a supernatural source. It cannot be derived from external conditions or from our emotional status. We cannot "work ourselves" into contentment or will it to be so. Contentment is not an emotion, a negotiation or the ability to simply ignore what is taking place around us; neither is it a bare-knuckled, "grin and bear it" attitude. Contentment is found in the person of Jesus Christ. It is the state of abiding within the very presence of Jesus and of allowing Him to reign within our earthly circumstance. Whether the Lord desires for us to wait quietly in contentment or to brave rugged terrain or harsh environments in contentment; He is the source that provides the strength to do so. Contentment is the state of abiding within the very presence of Jesus and of allowing Him to reign within our earthly circumstance. He is the only true source of the needed peace or contentment that we seek while we sojourn through the difficulties of life or find ourselves at a standstill.

Jesus brings peace because He is peace; His name is peace (Isaiah 9:6). His provision of peace is available to each of us and in all of our life circumstances and situations. We must learn to bask in His presence regardless of our circumstances or surroundings if we desire to abide in true contentment and peace. It is only the disciple who has focused her gaze on Jesus who can be content and at peace while everything around her appears dead, futile, without hope or destitute and lacking sustenance. If we desire to dwell in contentment as Paul and Habakkuk claimed then we must change our focus and our spiritual dwelling place.

The contented disciple daughter will learn to dwell in the presence of the Most High God and find her shelter against the perils of life there (Psalm 91:1). She will quiet her emotions and listen with her heart to what the Spirit of God is telling her. She will learn to see with the eyes of faith and train her ears to recognize the song of triumph that has already begun. She will rest in the knowledge that the caravan of deliverance is moving through the desert even though she may not hear it and it may still seem far away. The victory over circumstance is ours to claim but we must learn how to be still and wait in contentment. Soon we will see the warriors and banners of our King. Soon He will spread a banqueting table before us and satisfy the deepest longing of our soul. Soon there will be a shoreline on the horizon and a wind to fill our sails.

Heart's Cry

Lord, give me the faith and the discipline to echo the words of Habakkuk and of Paul. I want to be content and at peace as I travel with you in and out of both pleasant and difficult situations. Help me to trust your hands to provide for my every need even when times are lean. Change my focus and help me to fix my eyes on Nissi and to the hills from whence comes my strength. Whether I wait in the valleys, in the fogs, or in the still of the deep teach me to hear the voice of my Shepherd with clarity and to follow only as He leads. Amen

Finding Life within the Tomb

Scripture Meditation

"And there was Mary Magdalene and the other Mary, sitting over against the sepulcher."(Matthew 27:61).

"Jesus wept."(John 11:35).

"...a time to weep and a time to laugh," (Ecclesiastes 3:4).

"Surely it was for my benefit that I suffered such anguish. In your love you kept me from the pit of destruction: you have put all my sins behind your back. For the grave cannot praise you, death cannot sing your praise; those who go down to the pit cannot hope for your faithfulness."(Isaiah 38:17-18).

"Comfort, comfort my people, says your God. Speak tenderly to Jerusalem, and proclaim to her that her sin has been paid for, and that she has received from the Lord's hand double for all her sins."(Isaiah 40:1-3).

Musing

There is a time for weeping; Scripture in Ecclesiastes tells us that. Weeping is often the only appropriate response to the pain and heartache that we feel. We are never forbidden by God's Word to weep or to express our true emotions. The Lord Jesus wept openly in front of the mourners gathered at the tomb of His friend Lazarus. We must never feel that we are to hide our true emotions, our pain or our hurt from our loving Father. But as we are bruised, broken and elected to suffer great pain we must remember the pain, suffering and bruising that Jesus elected to suffer on our behalf. He knows our pain and has suffered the grief of loss and heartache. He is our High Priest who can offer us mercy and grace in our time of need as one who sympathizes and as one who has experienced what we now experience (Hebrews 4:14-16). He prayed with loud anguish and offered up tears to His Father just as we now cry out in our pain (Hebrews5:7-10).

Sometimes we forget that Jesus was fully God and yet fully man. He lived a life housed in flesh and blood and as such He had friends and family, relatives and followers whom He loved and who loved Him in return (Hebrews 2:14). The pain that His family and followers felt upon seeing His humiliation and torture followed by His terrible and prolonged death was real. In the fleshly realm they had suffered the loss of a son, a leader, a teacher, a brother and a friend. And in His flesh, as Jesus prayed in the Garden of Gethsemane, He knew that His obedient death to His human life here on earth would mean the end to His earthly relationships and human interactions with the people whom He had grown to love. Never again would He know these people as He now knew them; but Jesus also knew that in His death as a son, a brother and a friend He was offering those whom He loved a Savior, a Redeemer, a Messiah and an Eternal King. He found the strength required to offer up His human life in torturous death because He knew that in doing so He would usher in eternal life not only those with whom He now interacted but for all mankind (John 3:16). His great love for His earthly friends compelled Jesus to surrender to the very real pain of crucifixion and to the humiliation of the cross (John 15:13). There could be no greater display of love for His friends than to freely offer up His life on their behalf. Remember as you read these words that Jesus calls you His friend and that you are counted among those for whom He died.

I believe that our Creator wants us to experience our emotions and to look at our feelings. He just doesn't want us to look *with* our feelings or allow them to define our circumstances. Our God designed us with emotions and wants us to look at our emotions, to acknowledge them and to know them as we then choose to fix our thoughts on Jesus, our High Priest. We can tether our emotions by remembering that Christ was faithful to fulfill His calling despite experiencing the very real human emotions of grief, anguish and heartache (Hebrews 3:1-6). Our Father wants us to bring our emotions captive, to line them up in agreement with the truth of His Word, and to then allow the mind of Christ and the attitudes of the Holy Spirit to rule over those emotions (1 Corinthians 2:9-16, 2 Corinthians 5:7). By doing this, we can walk in discernment, and in faith, even when we are grief stricken and in pain. We will be guided by truth rather than blinded by our raw emotions and anguish.

The women who had come to dress the dead body of Jesus after His crucifixion were dealing with very real grief and pain. They had come to visit their once living messiah in a place of death. This tomb where Jesus was laid was a place in which death reigned supreme and in which only heartache and mourning lived. Their grief was only compounded when they entered His tomb and learned that the dead body they had come to attend was not there. The women were troubled by the *missing dead body* of Jesus. They were unable to think of any other explanation for the empty tomb. The human emotions experienced by these women blinded them and caused them to forget the words that Jesus spoke when He promised that He would resurrect. They did not remember and thus dared not to dream of a living Lord in this place of death.

Mary's interpretation of the missing *dead* body was that someone had taken it in an act of foul play, disrespect and mischief. As a result of these incorrect assumptions that were guided by her emotions Mary suffered even greater turmoil and pain (John 20:2-13). Mary's emotions did not allow her to see the situation from a point of faith. If she had been able to do so, she would have remembered Jesus' promise and looked for His *living* body rather than grieve over a missing *dead* one. Sadly, we are not unlike Mary when we become blinded by the pain or heartache of our daily living. We fail to look for hope in the midst of what we interpret as absolute despair and do not see life in the presence of death. Continuing to see with eyes of faith in such circumstances would be counter intuitive to all reasoning, emotion, culture and conventional thinking. When we surrender to what our emotions see rather than stand in the knowledge of what our God says, our faith becomes blinded and we fail to believe the possibility of our Father's promises.

If we would learn to look with our eyes of faith and to interpret our situations utilizing God's understanding then what appears to be an instrument of grief, heartache and pain can be used by the Father for our good and become a vital part of His overall plan (Genesis 50:20). Mary failed to see that what she was experiencing was all a part of God's wonderful plan of salvation. She did not know that she had been given the honor of being eye witness to God's power over death. She stood there alone in the tomb's garden blinded by her grief and unaware that the risen Lord was about to commission her as the first missionary to bring the good news of the gospel to the entire world (John 20:18).

While the grieving followers of the Lord forgot His words of promised resurrection, His enemies remembered them well and heeded them as a cautionary tale (Matthew 27:63-66). The religious and political leaders who were responsible for carrying out the crucifixion of Jesus took extra precautions as they blocked His tomb with a large boulder and set an armed guard at its mouth. They reasoned a bolder and around the clock security to be impossible barriers for any of Christ's followers wishing to pull off a hoax by removing His body and spreading a rumor that He had resurrected as he proclaimed. What these religious leaders failed to recognize is that our God uses what seems to be insurmountable circumstances to accomplish His miraculous plans.

Joseph was sold by his brothers, thrown into prison, lied about by Potiphar's wife, and then thrown into prison yet a second time (Genesis, chapters 37-40). It was during Joseph's second imprisonment that Pharaoh heard of his ability to interpret dreams and summoned him to reveal the meanings of the dreams that were disturbing his sleep. Joseph gained Pharaoh's trust and was placed in a position of authority over all of Egypt (Genesis, chapter 41). From his position of authority Joseph was able to provide for his brothers and their families during a time of great famine and became the instrument of God's grace to the tribes of Israel (Genesis 50:15-19). The impossible became the vehicle of the Almighty and was used to accomplish His great purpose.

When we are filled with grief and overcome with despair we must not allow it to blind us to the truth or to drag us into the pit of depression and defeat (Isaiah 38: 17-18). We must cling to the reassurance of God's promises of victory over death and of newness of life (Revelation 1:18). The Lord is all knowing. What seems senseless or cruel in our rationale can be used for His glory. We can trust that our Father knows what is best and that He is working all things, even our present pain and difficulty, together for our good (1 Samuel 3:18, Romans 8:28). As His daughters, we have His promise to provide us with hope and with a blessed future (Jeremiah 29:11). Even as we walk through a wide gulf of despair or a time of wilderness and wanton emptiness, we have the assurance that our God will never leave us or forsake us and that He is leading us out (Psalm 23:4,Hebrews 13:5). It is also good to remember while we travail that though Jesus was called the "Man of Sorrows", He overcame the world. Even death could not hold the Lord and by His power it cannot defeat those who trust in His name. Look for the risen Lord in the midst of your grief and pain. He is there.

Heart's Cry

Father, in this time of trial and of great pain, I pray that I would be submissive and patient and able to trust that you are working even this to your glory and for my benefit. Help me to hold fast to your promise of newness of life and of a hope and a future even while I am in pain and blinded by my grief. Equip me to trust just a little longer while traveling through this wide wilderness in which you have called me. Do not allow me to go down into the grave or the pit of depression and despair or to wallow in self-pity. Do not allow bitterness or anger to overtake me. Deliver me and use this trial as an instrument of your grace and my further refining. Amen

Protecting Ourselves from Identity Theft

Scripture Meditation

"The boys grew up, and Esau became a skillful hunter, a man of the open country, while Jacob was content to stay at home among the tents. Isaac, who had a taste for wild game, loved Esau, but Rebekah loved Jacob. Once when Jacob was cooking some stew, Esau came in from the open country, famished. He said to Jacob, "Quick, let me have some of that red stew! I'm famished!" (That is why he was also called Edom.) Jacob replied, "First sell me your birthright" "Look, I am about to die," Esau said. "What good is the birthright to me?" But Jacob said, "Swear to me first." So he swore an oath to him, selling his birthright to Jacob. Then Jacob gave Esau some bread and some lentil stew. He ate and drank, and then got up and left. So Esau despised his birthright."(Genesis 25:29-34).

"You belong to your father, the devil, and you want to carry out your father's desires. He was a murderer from the beginning, not holding to the truth, for there is no truth in him. When he lies, he speaks his native language, for he is a liar and the father of lies."(John 8:44).

"Then you will know the truth, and the truth will set you free."(John 8:32)

Musing

Citizens traveling abroad, whether for business or for fun, risk identity theft simply because they are traveling within an unknown region and within unfamiliar territory. Laws and customs may be quite different than what they are back home and by necessity travelers carry several pieces of sensitive information such as a passport, bank cards, driver's license, and an assortment of additional documents that could put them at risk if lost or stolen. Of course, when we are traveling, it's also easy to forget that not everyone is our friend and that some people have ulterior motives.

Savvy travelers know how important it is to heed travel alerts and warnings regarding the particular country in which they are traveling and conducting business as well as the need to keep documents secure against any person who would want to steal their identity and leave them away from home without any proof of citizenship or evidence to support their claims. Travelers must be ever vigilant as focus can be quickly lost when sensibilities become overwhelmed by the sights and sounds of the festivities taking place around them or when they are enticed by the sweet aromas of the delicacies now being offered them. This is especially true when a traveler is exhausted or suffering from jet lag and after they have endured a long period of hunger.

The above cautions can also be applied to any disciple daughter who finds that she is traveling through the enemy's territory or crossing through a wide wilderness of want. Many naïve sojourners of the Lord have fallen prey to the villainous crime of identity theft due to their lack of caution and unawareness of the enemy's snares. We become especially vulnerable to these attacks when we are tired, emotionally stretched, or suffering from a lack of proper nutrition.

Perhaps a few of us who are familiar with the story of the two brothers Jacob and Esau have piously judged Esau during previous readings of his account. It does seem utterly ridiculous that any grown man would be stupid enough to forfeit his birthright for what amounts to a bowl of beans. That birthright represented Esau's future security and the security of all his descendants who would come behind him. While it is true that this entitlement could be forfeited or withdrawn upon the committing of any serious sin; it would be unheard of for a young man to surrender his inheritance and future for something as frivolous as the desire to fill his stomach. The birthright of the eldest son gave him preference over his younger brothers, authority in his father's household and the assurance of a double portion from his father's estate at the time of his father's death. It could also be used as a bartering tool as is the case in the story of the two brothers. Jacob and Esau both understood the value and importance of a Jewish man's birthright when Esau swore an oath to his manipulating trickster brother to give up his inheritance and right to a double portion in exchange for what amounted to a bowl of red lentil stew.

If we pause for just a moment and get honest with ourselves, some of us might have to confess that often times we are not much different than Esau. Many times while traveling across the Wide Wilderness of Want we have been tricked into trading our identity and birthright as daughters of the King of Kings and heirs to his estate for what doesn't amount to any more than "a hill of beans" either. We trade our birthright to fill a momentary desire or lust and surrender our identity to the lies, myths, half-truths and traditions of the culture in which we are now conducting business on our Father's behalf. Much like Esau we reason that we are hungry now (verse 32) and convince ourselves just as he did that we will die if we do not have the enticement being offered or obtain the object of our desires. We convince ourselves of the urgency to feed the hunger and fleshly desire of the moment and determine to worry about the future if and when it arrives. After all, what good is a future birthright and inheritance going to do us now in this wanton situation if we die before we actually receive it?

As Ambassadors of the King of kings we need to be very careful about how flippant we are with the blessings and authority of our position. Scripture compares the action taken by Esau to that of sexual immorality (Hebrews 12:16). He was worldly and materialistic and traded in something of eternal and immeasurable value in order to satisfy a physical desire or momentary fleshly hunger. If we are not wise and do not guard our hearts from the enticements of the enemy we may be tripped up by the same temptations and led away by our sinful lusts (Ephesians 5:1-15).

Our enemy's greatest crime against the women of God is identity theft. It happens each time we begin to evaluate our worth utilizing a bean counting system of his devising. Each time that we measure our value using numbers such as those found on the bathroom scale, on the tag in the back of our jeans, on our bank statements or in the square footage of our house we forfeit a small portion of who we are in Christ Jesus. Sadly too many of us secure our value in these numbers and become confused regarding our true identity and value as established in our relationship with our Lord.

If we continue trading in our birthright to satisfy our immediate need to measure up or to belong in this foreign land, we could end up just like Esau: despising our birthright, tricked out of our inheritance, *and* missing our double portion.

Remember it is the truth that sets us free and secures us as we travel through the Wilderness of Want. Knowing the truth of who we are in Christ Jesus is foundational to our ability to stand against the lies and half-truths that are daily being hurled at us. We must be wary of any gain or enticement offered by our enemy as Scripture describes him as the "father of all lies" (John 8:44). Each traveler needs to have a ready arsenal of Scripture verses available as documented proof to verify our identity and value to the Lord. These can also be used to rebuke the enemy and to expose his lies. These verses will be life giving and affirm our faith when we feel shaky, fearful, or otherwise insecure within our present location or surroundings.

Speaking the truth to ourselves and about ourselves will help us to avoid taking on the burden of the weight that our enemy's lies produce. Avoiding the burden of these lies will require that all of the inward thoughts and conversations line up with the truth of Scripture. Our mulley grubbing and wallowing in self-loathing or self-pity has to cease as well. All of our fleshly desires and idols of want must be cast aside and our condemning conversation has to submit to the truth of God's Word. If we are to survive the Wide Wilderness of Want then our thoughts, motivations, and words must line up with the truth and authority of Scripture. Anything that we think, say, or hear about ourselves that doesn't line up with what God says is *a lie*. It must be bound and placed at the feet of Christ Jesus. Scripture reminds us that out of the overflow of the heart the mouth speaks (Luke 6:45). The contents of our heart provides the wellspring of life therefore we need to guard it carefully (Proverbs 4:23). The thought patterns of the daughter who is traveling through the wilderness must be true, pure, lovely and admirable (Philippians 4:8). Her attitude must be identical to that of Christ Jesus (Philippians 2:5). She must also train her tongue to confess that Jesus is Lord and that she belongs to him. In this way, she will reflect her Father while relying upon the work of the Holy Spirit to daily transform her into a truer reflection of him. Utilizing these tactics will carry every disciple daughter victoriously through her time of discontent and want.

Since being cast out of heaven, our enemy's number one objective has been to trip up, to hold captive and to defeat the ambassadors of God. He seeks to do so by perverting God's truth in the hopes that this will isolate us from our loving Father and leave us helpless and destitute in our sin (Genesis 3:4-5, 2 Corinthians 11:3). Our enemy recognizes that when we are separated from the truth of the love of our Father we become vulnerable to his enticements and are more easily lured away by our fleshly desires. Therefore, it is imperative for every precious daughter of the King who is traveling through a time of wilderness or of want to secure her identity in Him. She must also firmly establish an unshakable knowledge of her heavenly Father's great and unconditional love for her. Doing so will stop the enemy dead in his tracks and prevent a spirit of abandonment from leading us into sin.

Victorious disciple daughters know who they are and trust their identity to the truth of Christ Jesus. He is their sustenance and sufficiency as they cross through this Wide Wilderness of Want. Trusting His provision leaves them in need of nothing and prevents them from selling their birthright for a momentary enticement and from becoming the victim of identity theft.

Heart's Cry

Father remind me of who I am in you. Help me to demolish every thought, imagination or argument that is contrary to the truth and authority of your Word. Establish your will and purpose for my life as the primary focus for my motivations. Continue your restorative work of refinement and transform me into vessel set aside for your service. Amen.

Seeking

*Lord, teach me to desire to know **who you are***
*rather than to seek **what you do**.*
*To be **in you** rather than **to do for** you.*
This is my desire for herein will I find contentment and obtain victory.
Draw me closer still.

Amen

Not Alone

Scripture Meditation

"...And surely I am with you always, to the very end of this age."(Matthew 28:20b).

"Even though I walk through the valley of the shadow of death, I will fear no evil for you are with me; your rod and your staff they comfort me."(Psalm 23:4).

"Neither height, nor depth, nor anything else in all creation will be able to separate us from the love of God that is in Christ Jesus our Lord."(Romans 8:39).

"For God is not a God of disorder but of peace."(1 Corinthians 14:33).

Musing

Our God desires to be with us in the extremes of our lives and to share our valleys as well as on the mountain tops. He longs to be present in the depths of despair and of driest desert as well as in the times of greatest joy and celebration as we are poised at the pinnacle of our achievement and success. He promises to be the God who will never leave us or forsake us. He is bigger than our biggest problem, deeper than our deepest despair and more powerful than our most powerful foe or fear. He is able to meet us where we are and to supply our every need whether that need be physical, mental or spiritual. The God who sustains all that exists within the palms of His hands also holds each of His children in the very place where they presently abide. We are forever in His presence and He will answer when we call.

Genesis chapter 16 recounts the story of Hagar, the Egyptian maidservant of Sarai the wife of the Patriarch Abraham. After Sarai became jealous over Hagar's pregnancy, which was conceived due to Sarai's manipulative deception and doubt of God's word; she mistreated Hagar and caused Hagar to flee into the wilderness. In the middle of that great desert where Hagar sat she had an encounter with God at a spring of running water. Hagar referenced this God who had previously been unknown to her with the name "*El Roi*". This name has been translated to mean that God had seen her in her plight and that *likewise she had seen Him* while in the midst of her trial and tribulation (Genesis 16: 13-14). In that first desert meeting El-Roi shared His plan for Hagar's life with her. She then did as God had instructed and returned to the house of Sarai to give birth to Ishmael (Genesis 16:15). At this point, readers might be inclined to think that because Hagar obeyed the Lord and went back to her mistress everything went well in her life from there but this was not the case.

Further along in the book of Genesis we read that after Hagar returned from her desert encounter Sarai continued to be jealous and bitter against her and subsequently Abraham released Hagar and her teenage Son from his household and cut them off from any rightful inheritance (Genesis 21:8-11). It was Sarai's bitterness against Hagar for being pregnant with Abraham's child that forced her out into the desert for that first time, and now Sarai's continued jealousy over Hagar's teenage son forced them both out of the only home they had known. For a second time Hagar found herself wandering in the desert sobbing and crying out to God (Genesis 21:15). This time, as in the past, God heard her cries along with the cries of her dying son and intervened on her behalf. He met their immediate needs and fulfilled His greater plan for each of their lives and for all the descendants of Abraham (Genesis 21:17-21).

When the desert of despair becomes our dwelling place, we must be willing to listen for and to see our God there in the midst. We have the promise that we will pass through this difficulty if we will listen intently for the Shepherd's voice and find our comfort in the assurance of His presence. Training our ears to hear God's voice while exiled in the wilderness or enduring the pain of stripping (death) teaches us the discipline of being still and of knowing that He alone is God. Though our present circumstances may be difficult and our treatment may seem harsh and unjust, we do not need to fear our Father's touch or His correction (His rod and staff). We do not need to fear that He has forsaken or abandoned us in our trouble. Our God is present. He meets us with a Father's heart and approaches us with everlasting, unconditional love. He is bound to His children in covenant agreement and sees us as His beloved daughters.

When we are willing to look unto the Lord in our harshest and driest places of testing and isolation, He will share His vision and His secret thoughts. He will expose the source of any confusion by the light of His steadfast Word and strengthen our dying faith through the assurance of His spoken promises. He will look upon us with favor as He opens up a storehouse of treasures greater than any earthly inheritance to supply our every need. He will restore our inheritance to us. Just as God provided a stream in the desert for Hagar and a well of water for her dying son; so He will keep His promises to His beloved children and regenerate us with His streams of living water. He will bind up our wounds and anoint us there in His presence. He will be our peace as He sends us onward with His commission. We are not abandoned and we are not alone.

Heart's Cry

Lord, go with me now as I cross over the hills and through the valleys of my daily living. Help me to keep my eyes on you and to see you as my sufficiency though I travel through the wilderness of want. Allow me to see you in the midst of my dry places and difficult situations. Make your presence known to me Father, and teach me to rest assured in the knowledge that I am not alone. Accomplish what you desire in me and through me in this time of testing and lead me out at the approved time as your appointed ambassador and beloved daughter. Amen

Becoming Anointing Oil

Scripture Meditation

"Is there no balm in Gilead? Is there no physician there? Why then is there no healing for the wounds of my people?"(Jeremiah 8:22).

"Praise be to the God and Father of our Lord Jesus Christ, the Father of compassion who comforts us in all our troubles so that we can comfort those in in any trouble with the comfort we ourselves have received from God."(2 Corinthians 1:3-4).

"You anoint my head with oil; my cup runneth over."(Psalm 23:5b).

"They came to Bethsaida, and some people brought a blind man and begged Jesus to touch him."(Mark 8:22).

Musings

When our faith is stretched to the point of supreme stress due to the circumstances in which we presently find ourselves and even as we feel that we are at an end and are weary; that our bones are brittle and that our hearts are so heavy and sore that they cannot possibly bear any more, we can rest assured that we will not break or crumble. Contrary to what our emotions may be screaming, God has not brought us to this place of testing and tribulation to destroy us or to leave us here to die (Deuteronomy 4:31). He has brought us to this wilderness and to the end of self in order to cause us to reach out to the beginning of Him. He desires for us to let go of our temporary riches in order to give us an eternal inheritance that cannot be destroyed. He longs for us to unclench our fists and to release the worldly things that we hold so tightly to in order to grasp hold of Him. He desires to be merciful toward His children and everything that touches our lives is filtered through His unconditional love and grace (1 John 3:1). Though the wilderness in which we now dwell may seem hostile and our traveling be arduous we can rest in the full knowledge that our Father is working this very moment for our good and for His express purpose (Romans 8:28).

Our Father desires to comfort us in the midst of this tribulation and to refine us with this trial. He will not leave us comfortless, abandoned or orphaned in this desert (Hebrews 13:5, John 14:18). Even as our heart aches and we are down-trodden, wounded, or oppressed; He is the gentle physician (Jeremiah 17:5-8). His name is *Jehovah-Rapha*. It is by His stripes and His suffering that we are made physically, mentally and spiritually whole (Isaiah 53:4). Our faith will not be destroyed nor will we be cut down by the enemy if we will allow the healing balm of His anointing to keep us pliable in His hands and flexible in our faith even while in the midst of this great stripping and stretching. We can trust even now in His steadfast love and never failing faithfulness. He is our salvation, our sufficiency and our deliverance.

Even while the pressure of this hard place causes our souls to despair and stretches our faith it is our Father's desire that it would lead us into His throne room. He longs for us to boldly call out to be given more of His anointing oil and healing touch as lift our emptying cups up for His blessing and for a fresh filling. He will lavishly pour a fresh supply over us and immerse us in His rivers of mercy and streams of grace. Even the harshest wilderness and driest desert can become a place of healing and an oasis of renewal when we surrender up our wills and confess an end to all self- reliance. We must confess to our Father that cannot do this thing alone and recognize that we will not endure the walk through this barren wilderness even another step without the Shepherd to lead and His grace to sustain us. It is then that He becomes the source of living water and the sufficiency for that which our soul now thirsts (John 4:10-14). We become victorious when we remember that Christ overcame all things and it is in His name and through His authority that we lay claim to our presently unattained and yet unseen victory (John 16:33, Romans 8:37).

Our times of trial and places of desert heat are of heavenly design and godly orchestration. God has purposed this place of dryness and thirst as a place for anointing, for reproof, for refining and for consecration unto

Him. The great leader Moses was exiled alone on the back side of the desert when he met with God and received his call to ministry (Exodus 3). God had taken him into the desert and removed him from the luxuries of palace life. He was stripped of his title and social position and subjugated to the duties of sheep herder when he came to that place of seeing God in the burning bush. So it is with us. God often gets us alone and takes away the distraction of luxury and the clamor of social activity to begin the process of refinement and of deeper revelation.

Our time in the wilderness is oftentimes used as a place of preparation and equipping. For example, it was while exiled in that desert wilderness tending his father in law's sheep that Moses learned how to daily endure the heat of the sun. This was in preparation for the long years that he would spend leading God's wandering human sheep through the desert under that same blistering heat. Moses learned how to lead stubborn and witless sheep in preparation for his call to lead the stubborn and quickly distracted Children of Israel. He also learned to see God's presence and to know God's voice. Moses learned humility and developed a servant's heart by tending sheep. He learned perseverance and patience by working diligently to receive his father in law's blessing.

Our time of desert dryness and of stretching is not purposed for our good alone but serves to benefit others as well. When we have learned to see God's presence in our sorrow and to trust His character in our trial then we are able to testify to the truth of His comfort and deliverance to others. The healing and fragrant oil only pours forth after the olive has been crushed and it is after we have endured trial and suffering that we become a healing balm and soothing oil to be used by the Father. We are available to be poured out into the lives of those around us who now endure similar despair and pain. How can we speak with assurance of God's healing touch if we have never felt it? How can we speak of His comfort and of His great love if we do not know it? We can only speak of faith that is stretched and of hope that endures *after* we have known and overcome such testing for ourselves.

It is after we have walked through our desert time that we can become a Moses in the lives of others. After we have been tested and stretched and have passed through victoriously to the other side we can lead others to the deliverance of our Savior. We can bring those around us to the Lord for His restoring and healing touch just as the blind man's friends brought him (Mark 8:22). Jesus knows what others need and we know how to help them find Him. We know what it is to hurt and to wait in silence and despair; but more importantly we know that God answers prayer and that though the night seems long, joy **will** return in the morning.

Heart's Cry

Jesus be my physician and my daily bread in this hour and in this situation. I come boldly into your presence now, Father, and call your attention to me in my hour of discouragement and despair. Deliver my answer directly from your throne room. Immerse me in your living waters through the presence of your Holy Spirit. Heal me from my battle wounds and fill me with the grace and mercy needed to continue to be pliable and flexible as clay in your hands. Use me in ministry to others. As I surrender to your touch, may I become a comforting balm and soothing oil in the lives of those around me. Amen

Surrender

Broken Bread...
Poured Out Wine...
Healing Oil...
Feed corn.
Crushed Olive...
Bruised Reed...
Willing servant...
Buried seed.
Surrendered Life, yielded and still.
Father I come, show me your will.

The Muddled Fogs of Confusion and Doubt

The disciple daughter was a bit befuddled and confused to discover, after making her way through the tangled branches and briers of the wilderness, that she was now surrounded by a dense blanket of wet fog. This heavy air clouded all ability to decipher anything beyond her fingertips, blinded her eyes and greatly distorted her judgment. Everything around her was draped in shadows as she sat enveloped within a dense and dark feeling of despair. The weary pilgrim honestly had no idea that she would still be traveling after what seemed such a long passage of time. The Shepherd wasn't leading where she had hoped and, if she were being honest, the traveler would have to confess to being exasperated with Him. He did not seem to grow weary with the languishing passage of time and simply wasn't responding in the timeframe or manner that she had expected.

Rather than be excited over the possibility of experiencing new places and learning new things, the disciple had grown bored with the continual expanse of desert sand and then exhausted by the twisting trails of the wilderness. Travel in the territories that she had just passed through had proven to be slow and tedious for the disciple daughter. She had to be ever vigilant as each leg of her journey was wrought with the threat of real danger. She dealt with the intense heat of the sun's direct rays and the constant shifting of the sands under her feet while crossing through The Desert of Transition; then had to constantly be on the lookout for falling branches and gnarled roots as she made her way through the Wilderness of Want. She also had to closely monitor every step as the oil lamp that the Shepherd provided in the wilderness cast only enough light to see directly up ahead. Now, after all of her trials and tribulations, the exasperated and somewhat short-tempered disciple sat perched and pouting on what appeared to be a high cliff or a rocky ledge. Though she did not seem to be any nearer to her Father's dwelling place, she tried to muster up strength by imagining that the King's mighty towers were closer than she knew; after all, she couldn't be quite sure of anything with all the fog that had settled in.

The source of the exasperated traveler's current disposition stemmed from the fact that neither the Father, the Shepherd nor her guide was doing what she wanted done when or how she imagined. She had no sense of control over her wanderings and had no idea how much longer this sojourn would continue. Now, to make matters worse, the thick blanket of fog was blinding her to everything around her. It also sometimes aggravated the disciple daughter that none of her heavenly traveling companions shared her impatient temperament and seemed to measure the passage of time differently. They never moved in a hurried pace or appeared the least bit discouraged by the limited vision or never- ending traveling. While the disciple became impatient with the Father's limited disclosure of His plans and frustrated over the seemingly serendipitous nature of their course; the others trusted Him completely and did not need to know anything beyond the information that the Father provided. The Shepherd could lie down and rest in the strangest of places and never seemed concerned over the weather, the difficulty of the terrain, or the depletion of their supplies. At one point she could not help but wonder if the Shepherd had heard correctly or whether the Father had actually chosen the best route for their journey. The path that they followed seemed so circuitous and winding. On more than one occasion the disciple daughter was certain that she had passed by a particular obstacle or landmark earlier and was simply traveling past it yet again. Certainly the all-knowing Father could have designed a more direct route through the wilderness. He also could have easily removed all the obstacles that blocked her path and exposed all the roots that kept tripping her up. He did forewarn her of their existence but she still had to be vigilant to avoid faltering.

The embittered daughter could not understand why she was now sitting alone in this muddled fog after enduring stubbed toes, twisted ankles, and scraped knees. She was discouraged and confused by the Father's response to her faithful perseverance, dedication, and commitment. She also could not help but wonder how long it would be before these clouds of confusion parted and the heavy fogs that dampened her spirit lifted. The disciple daughter began to grumble to herself regarding the unfairness of her present situation; after all, she had not feared the Lord's calling to come away and set out without question on the path of His choosing; and while it may have taken her some time, she did complete her traverse across the desert and through the wilderness. She reasoned that her actions surely had to count for something and wondered why the Father wasn't here offering congratulations on her success thus far. The Father appeared to be uncaring, distant and silent, and His disciple daughter failed to understand any of His movements right now. She lacked clarity regarding His present dealings with her and falsely judged Him to be ambivalent rather than loving. The disciple had even begun to question the Father's wisdom as she knew that if she had been given control of things her present situation would have been much different.

The now disenchanted sojourner sadly remembered how she had once traveled in heightened expectation feeling certain that glorious things were about to happen around every corner. This expectant feeling faded and she began to grow discouraged with the drudgery of too many mundane days spent with the shepherd. These were quickly followed with other days that were trying beyond measure and difficult beyond comparison. She could not recall anyone at any time in her days at home warning her that following the Shepherd would be like this. She also didn't recall learning that the life of a disciple would be filled with more ordinary days spent down in the valley than days filled with miracles and spent on the mountain top. Her guide had promised that if she would come away on this journey the Father would reveal great and unsearchable things that she did not currently know. She questioned how He planned to accomplish that by plotting her journey through mundane and ordinary valleys most days only to then follow up with days that left her in utter exhaustion.

The disciple daughter had followed the Shepherd hoping for a great adventure. She wanted the extraordinary experiences of the mountain top and the views and the vistas from the Father's dwelling place. From her present perspective things simply did not make sense. It would be impossible to know the supernatural touch of the creator of the universe while living and traveling among the ordinary things of everyday life. Her melancholy grew and disappointment increased as she longed for clearer vision and hungered and thirsted for the deeper things of God. She wanted the Father to meet her as He had never met her before and dreamt of a life that transcended the monotony and the routine of normalcy. She had prayed that the Father would be grand in her presence and that He would do great things both in and through her. Now, she sat alone and in despair in the clouds and in the middle of nowhere.

The weary traveler needed renewed vision and hope if she were going to continue on this journey. She needed for this fog to lift just long enough for her to regain reassurance of her Father's guidance. The Father's silence coupled with her inability to see Him was making it increasingly difficult for her to hold fast to the sort of faith that overcomes and perseveres in any and all circumstances. Such faith was particularly hard to find now when everything around her was clouded and confused. Perhaps if she could just see the Father's dwelling place in the distance then she would know that this was the path that He had designated for her. That would be sign enough to restore her faith. The disciple daughter squinted her eyes together tightly and strained to peer beyond the heavy clouds in the hopes of seeing her Father's towers and thus receiving rational substantiation for her faith's existence. It was no use; everything was blanketed and obscured.

The traveler tried to understand why the Father had allowed such doubt and confusion to cross her path and to obscure her vision. Did He suppose that she would continue to trust the Shepherd's leading even when the way seemed so unclear? How could she continue to have faith in a Father whose ways she did not understand and in a guide who seemed to be communicating in puzzles and riddles rather than in open disclosure? She wondered why the Father was keeping so much hidden from her.

She longed for her guide to explain things in an honest and intimate way; after all, it was his job to teach her the secret things of God. Surely, he recognized her need to understand the Father's purpose for leaving her to sit here in this place of clouds. The disciple tried being still to allow the Father an opportunity to explain things to her. She stopped her pacing about and tried to settle her spirit. She listened for His still, small voice above the clouds and the fog; but all remained silent. The silence left the disciple daughter's spirit unsettled and her soul ill at ease. She knew that a relationship could not grow when communication was blocked. She wondered where her guide had gone as she could no longer feel His comforting presence. She also grew more and more fearful of the devourer that waited just outside her hiding place. She swore that she could hear his heavy footsteps pacing just beyond the Cave of Doubt's entrance.

As she sat pressed against the walls of that deep cave the disciple daughter's singing was quieted and her praise silenced. She tried praying and cried out to the Father from within her cave of doubt but even as she earnestly pleaded, her words seemed to get lost in the clouds and her fervor dissipated within the heaviness that the blanket of fog produced. Everything rang hollow as it bounced off the walls and echoed through the cavernous maze of doubt and despair in which she now hid herself away. The disciple could no longer hear the Shepherd's voice or decipher His call. She strained to listen but the cries of her own aching flesh grew louder as did the low growl of the enemy who seemed be to encroaching ever closer. She nervously peered about wondering if his stealthy movement had actually allowed him to enter her cave of doubt totally undetected. Fear was beginning to overtake her and she knew that if she were ever going to clear the wool from her eyes and the doubt from her heart then she needed to hear her Shepherd's voice. Sadly, the heavy fog muffled all sound and the disciple daughter sat alone in the dark and thankless in the deafening silence.

Contemplation

"Borrowed troubles do not exist until I bring them into my presence. They remain abstract until I give them weight and form and dedicate space to their existence. Worry and doubt have no power over me until I yield to their authority. Fear becomes a prison cell only if I willingly enter into it. Choosing to dwell in the land of the *If… then* rather than in the land of *what…if* will keep these imagined enemies of my faith far from my thinking and sustain me though my times of doubt. I must choose to bring all these thoughts captive to the Lord and to acknowledge His truth as my dwelling place."

Having done all... Stand

Scripture Meditation

"Finally, be strong in the Lord and in his mighty power. Put on the full armor of God, so that you can take your stand against the devil's schemes."(Ephesians 6:10-11).

"If you do not stand firm in your faith, you will not stand at all."(Isaiah 7:9b).

"He is like a tree planted by streams of water, which yields its fruit in season and whose leaf does not wither. Whatever he does prospers"(Psalm 1:3).

"-if you continue in your faith, established and firm, not moved from the hope held out in the gospel…"(Colossians 1:23a).

Musing

Tall trees require strong roots that press down deeply into the heart of the earth and dig beyond the surface of the ground in order to stand against the pressures of time, the weight of heavy rains and the blast of winter's gales. In order for their tall branches to canopy boldly and reach upward into the heavens they must be nourished and sustained by nutrients carried up from the sources of a fertile planting. This means that as young saplings they must have rich soil in which to begin the process of establishing their footing. Only then can these budding beauties grow into mighty oaks and graceful willows growing beside babbling rivers, bearing fruit and providing shelter and shade from the mid-day heat.

As mature Christians we are called to stand in faith when the storms of life seem to prevail against us. We are asked to maintain our stamina in times of spiritual drought and absence of comfort. We are asked to root ourselves firmly in the solid fact that God is in control and to dig deeply into the truth of His Word when our life predicaments seem to be in a state of chaos or confusion. We are asked to bear up when our enemy is bearing down and to be sure of the God in whom we hope and certain of the covenant promises which we do not presently see fulfilled (Hebrews 11:1).

The Lord asks us to stand firmly rooted in the facts of our faith and to respond to our circumstances utilizing His Spirit of power, love and self-discipline (2 Timothy 1:7). We are to arm ourselves with the truth of who we are in Christ Jesus and to recognize that no life situation; no matter how difficult or dire, can separate us from the love that our Father has for us (Romans 8:38). Staying rooted in the assurance of His love and sustained with the awareness of His power will bring us victory (Romans 8:35-37). If we stand upon the truth of our Father's Word as our foundation then we will remain upright against the most trying of temptation or trial because our enemy cannot defeat such a stance.

Our enemy seeks to destroy us and to devour our lives by cutting us off from our source and then tempting us to yield to his pressures (1 Peter 5:8-9). He howls like the wind attempting to uproot us and to toss us to and fro with his deceitfulness and crafty schemes (Ephesians 4:14). He desires for us to respond to our circumstances with fear, doubt and other destructive emotions rather than to operate in the fruits of the Holy Spirit (Galatians 5:22). We must choose instead to grow into Christ and to be joined together with Him and fully supported by His truth and His authority (Ephesians 4:15). Jesus is the true vine from whom all life giving energy flows (John 15:1-5). Only those branches that are grafted into Him receive nourishment and have strong anchor against the wind. Apart from His truth and His sovereign authority we cannot maintain life and will surely wither and die (John 15:6-7).

Christ is our sure foundation. He is our rock and our refuge (Isaiah 28:16). It is through Him that we are able to continue on in our faith and to be established firmly; unshakable and unmovable (Colossians 1:23). We can trust in our Savior though the wind sweeps through, the locust devours and the rain and hail beat down upon us. The depth of His great mercy, wisdom and knowledge will sustain us (Psalm 86:13,Romans 11:33-36). The one who trusts in God cannot be overtaken for He is before all things and it is in Him that all things are held together (Colossians 1:16). We must continue to live in Him, rooted and built up in Him and strengthened in the faith that we were taught (Colossians 2:6). This is how we stand.

Heart's Cry

Father, I ask that you would allow the words of Christ to dwell in me richly as you teach me how to anchor myself deeply in the knowledge of your Word and the hope of your promises. Make me alive in Christ and clothe me in His authority as I take my stand against the enemy and his tactics. Disarm him with your power, Lord, and strengthen my faith. I put my trust in you and know that in you I am victorious over all that the enemy might try to accomplish. Amen

Our High Priest is a "Man of Sorrows"

Scripture Meditation

"He was despised and rejected by men, a man of sorrows and familiar with suffering. Like one from whom men hide their faces, he was despised and we esteemed him not."(Isaiah 53:3).

"He was in the world, and though the world was made through Him, the world did not recognize him. He came to that which was his own, but his own did not receive him."(John 1:10-11).

"Coming to his home town, he began teaching the people in their synagogue and they were amazed. "Where did this man get this wisdom and these miraculous powers?" they asked. "Isn't his mother's name Mary, and aren't his brothers James, Joseph, Simon and Judas? Aren't his sisters with us? Where then did this man get all these things?" And they took offense at him."(Matthew 13:54-57).

"Jesus replied:" Foxes have holes and birds of the air have nests, but the Son of Man has no place to lay his head."(Luke 9:58).

"For we do not have a high priest who is unable to sympathize with our weaknesses, but we have one who has been tempted in very way, just as we are- yet was without sin. Let us approach the throne of grace with confidence so that we may receive mercy and find grace to help us in our time of need."(Hebrews 4:15-16).

Musing

Imagine the impact that believing with our whole being that our High Priest is like us in all manner and yet without sin could have on our prayer life and on our level of intimacy with God (Hebrews 4: 15). When life hurts, and it often does; we would know with full assurance that our God is all-loving, all-knowing and all compassionate. We would believe that our Father sees all that we are presently enduring and truly believe that our High Priest, Jesus, is able to understand our weakness and to sympathize with that which we experience.

Admittedly, it is difficult to comprehend at full depth what it means for Scripture to refer to the all-powerful and incarnate Son of God as the *Son of Man* and as "one who is familiar with human suffering" (Isaiah 53:3,Philippians 2:6-8,1 John 5:20). It is tempting to question how it could be that the infallible and sinless Son of God could know and feel what fallible and fallen people feel and almost impossible to accept that He who dwells in heaven could relate to the hurts and disappointments of those who walk on earth.

We can begin to believe in the empathy of our High Priest by realizing that the perfect Son of God was not removed from the world of flesh or protected from its hurts and disappointments. Jesus did not live a life cloistered away from the realities of daily human existence. He became flesh and dwelt among us (John 1:14). He left His throne and His Father's side to experience temporal life as we know it in the hopes of offering us eternal life and to show us that a fulfilled life on earth was only possible through Him (John 3:16,John 10:10).

Our Lord was not immune to the *human condition*. He saw poverty and sickness. He knew the heartache of grief and the sting of death. Scripture tells us that Jesus endured rejection, ridicule, being mocked and being judged and misunderstood as He traveled from town to town teaching (Matthew 22:22,Mark 1:22). Those in need oftentimes did not wish to hear what He had to say. How sad the Savior must have been to know that He had such good news to share while realizing that many would not listen. Jesus desired to unlock the great secrets and mysteries of His Father's kingdom through the parables that He taught yet many did not seek to understand (Acts 28:26-27). They wanted to experience His healing touch and to eat His free bread but they did not want to hear the truth that His Father sent Him to share.

I wonder how the Lord felt as His own family and those friends with whom He was most intimate looked at Him in disbelief and questioned

His authority (Matthew 13:53-58). He claimed to be the Son of God yet they saw nothing more than an ordinary carpenter's son who came from a nowhere town in the forgotten region of Galilee. Our High Priest knows what it is to be rejected. He knew what it was to be a man without a country or a home town. He told His disciples when they chose to follow Him that He did not even have a place here on earth to call His home (Luke 9:58).

Jesus also knew the rigors of spiritual warfare and understood the same stretching and testing that often causes us to want to give up. The same enemy that tempts us to sin and pressures us to turn our backs on our mission tempted and cajoled Him. Satan met Jesus in the wilderness and tried to dissuade Him from beginning His earthly ministry and from redeeming our salvation at the cross (Matthew 4:1-11). His enemy knew that it would be there on that cross that the sinless Son of God would take the sin of all mankind, endure total and absolute separation from His holy and loving Father, and purchase freedom for death's captives (Matthew 26:39-42,Matthew 27:45). Our High Priest bore it all. He knows how abandonment feels. On that cross Jesus endured the loneliness of being totally disowned by heaven and earth. He became an orphan on our behalf.

Our High Priest felt the sting of betrayal from those whom He trusted and who walked closely with Him. Judas Iscariot betrayed Jesus to the chief priests just to fill his purse with thirty pieces of silver (Matthew 26:14-16). Simon Peter, His most zealous disciple, betrayed Him three times as he cursed and shouted obscenities at those claiming that they had seen him with Jesus (Matthew 26:69-75). Even His three closest friends betrayed His confidence as they dozed off in sleep during Christ's greatest hour of sorrow and grief (Matthew 26:36-47). Not once, but three times, He begged His companions to wake up and to watch and pray with Him and three times He returned from His prayerful anguish and tears to find them napping. Our High Priest knows what it is to be disappointed by a close friend and to be betrayed by someone that we love. Jesus understands the depth of that hurt because He has experienced it firsthand.

Jesus knows the pain and loss of death. He experienced such grief at the death of His close friend, Lazarus (John 11:17-44). Our High Priest also knew as He watched His friend's sisters mourn that it was through His own death and resurrection that those who trusted in Him would find eternal life. He knew that His death would offer His followers the opportunity to rise in victory over death and the grave (1 Corinthians 15:50-57). What joy to know that Jesus died so that we would be free from the grief of an eternal death without hope (1 Thessalonians 4:13-18).

Even as Jesus openly wept with Mary and Martha at the graveside of Lazarus, He knew the hurt of false accusation and harsh judgment. He could hear the whispers and snide comments of those in the crowd gathered there as they questioned His motivations and falsely judged Him for not coming to Lazarus' home sooner. They ridiculed Him for failing to prevent Lazarus from dying (John 11:21,35,37). Our Lord knew the pain of gossip and other's hurtful whispers.

Our High Priest's heart sympathizes with our every grief. He understands our every pain. He has compassion on our weakness and remembers that we are formed of dust (Psalm 103:13-14). He is our gentle and loving savior who knows us and longs to meet our needs (Psalm 23). He is our blessed redeemer and our never tiring intercessor, our advocate and our friend. Our Lord will move toward us with compassion and mercy in our time of need. The Lord is qualified to forgive and to strengthen those who reach out to Him because He not only took on this life of flesh, but He endured it and passed every test, trial and temptation. He knows what we are going through and offers victory in every conflict. He knows our hurts and lovingly calls us His friend (John 15:9-17). Our High Priest offers us the full assurance that no matter what the temptation or the difficulty, He will never abandon us. He promises to stick closer than a brother (Hebrews 13:5,Proverbs 18:24). He is praying for His own and interceding before the Father's throne.

Our High Priest invites us to boldly present our heartaches, disappointments, and pain to Him. As God's beloved daughters we can have full confidence as we look into our Savior's face and tell our High Priest of our anguish. There is no need for trepidation, fear or worry over the response that will follow our request for help because our advocate is there and He loves us. What sweet fellowship we may have missed by refusing to believe that our Lord sincerely cares for us (1 Peter 5:7). What joy we may have forfeited by refusing to cast our cares upon Him and to lay our burdens at His feet. How vastly changed our walk would be if in our time of pain, despair, confusion or doubt we would remember the love of our Father, fall on His grace, and enter into His promised rest.

Heart's Cry

Oh Father God, to know that you did not spare your son in expressing your great love towards us is an awesome reality. Refresh my memory of all that he endured while walking this earth clothed in flesh. Help me to recall how very much you love me in my time of grief, disappointment, betrayal or exhaustion. Give me confidence to come to your throne of grace and to present my needs to my patient and sympathizing high priest and Lord. Thank you that I am your child and a rightful heir to the promises of the covenant that you established through Jesus. Let me enter into your rest today and find the strength and grace that I need. Amen

Housekeeping

My Child,

If you would see Jesus then begin in your heart.

Look deeply into the crevices, cobwebbed corners and dark recesses there.

If His light has not permeated those tiny little strongholds,

then throw back the draperies and allow it to enter now.

Saturate your spirit with newness of life.

Drink deeply from His grace and

allow His love to refresh, to renew, to rekindle and to regenerate your weary soul.

Let the truth of His love dispel all the shadows and fears and then

Bolt the door!

Cast out the enemy and allow him a foothold no longer.

Do not give him space even upon your doorstep.

Deliver up your heart's throne completely to the one who designed you.

Trust in His faithfulness as you follow His footsteps.

Hold out the sword of His Word as you forward into the night.

Rest secure in His shadow when darkness approaches.

Be assured-

He is present.

He is able to guide you and to keep you.

He is the light in which you now abide.

⚜ ⚜ ⚜

This too shall Pass

Scripture Meditation

"A happy heart makes the face cheerful, but heartache crushes the spirit. The discerning heart seeks knowledge, but the mouth of a fool feeds on folly."(Proverbs 13:14-15).

"A cheerful heart is good medicine, but a crushed spirit dries up the bones."(Proverbs 17:22).

"Speak to one another with psalms, hymns and spiritual songs. Sing and make music in your heart to the Lord, always giving thanks to God the Father for everything, in the name of Jesus Christ."(Ephesians 5:19-20).

"Why are you downcast, O my soul? Why so disturbed within me? Put your hope in God, for I will praise him my savior and my God. My soul is downcast within me; therefore I will remember you from the land of the Jordan, the heights of Hermon-from Mount Mizar."(Psalm 42:5-6).

"Oh the depth of the riches of the wisdom and knowledge of God. How unsearchable his judgments and his paths beyond tracing out."(Romans 11:33).

Musing

It is difficult to gauge one's progress when traversing through dense fogs of confusion and doubt. There are no landmarks, no mile markers and no trees or vegetation by which to determine how far one has traveled. There is no clear horizon in view that can be used to mark the journey's end. Everything is shrouded and dark; blanketed, socked in and never changing. Miles and miles of dense fog rolling on and on before a weary traveler can be discouraging and blinding. It obscures our ability to see the Shepherd's face and clouds our perspective (Proverbs 29:18). The oppressive thickness of the air labors our breathing as it suffocates all life and joy from within us. The weight of heaviness can make it difficult for us to move. Pressing onward in the thick darkness becomes frightening as the sharp chill of the air begins to parch our throats and crush our spirit… but we must persevere.

It is in times like these that we must remember that we only have a glimpse of all that God is doing. We see only a small portion of His activity and only the aspects of His plan that He has chosen to reveal. If we are to remain faithful, then we must ask God to give us the power to walk it out and the faith to keep going in spite of the darkness and shadows that surround us. We must ask for the childlike faith to trust and to obey and then look up to the countless stars in the heavens for the hope of our promise and the assurance of our covenant (Genesis 15:4, John 11:41). Childlike faith believes that the stars are there though we may not yet be able to see them. It also knows that God is working though we may not understand His leading. True faith trusts that the caravan is on the way and begins to sings the songs of thanksgiving even before seeing the fulfillment of God's promise (Genesis 37:25). It knows that the answer has already been obtained and the victory is won even while not yet seeing evidence to that fact within current physical surroundings.

Oh weary wanderer, if you can endure just a little while longer, you will see your promised destination. This time of questioning and insecurity will pass. Soon the clouds will part, the fog will lift and the sun will break through in divine revelation (Ecclesiastes 11:3). God will reveal His great mercy and joy over you with singing (Zephaniah 3:17).Though you may be weary now and your spirits may be dampened, soon renewing springs of living water will bubble forth from within you (John 7:38). There will be flowers and fruit in the meadow into which the Shepherd will lovingly lead you and there you will find rest. You will lie down beside a brook that babbles with praise. Birds will return to their nests and the fig tree will blossom. God will turn your valley of mourning into a meadow of blessing and joy (Psalm 84:5-6).

God will keep His promises if faith will patiently endure (Hebrews 6:15). Your victory is at hand as it is within your Father's hands (Habakkuk 3:17-18). The clouds will part and the sun will return to the sky. Wait a little longer ,disciple daughter, for joy will return with the morning.

Cinthia W. Pratt

Heart's Cry

Oh Father God, help me to look up when my soul is cast down and to have faith rather than to give in to the gloomy disposition of my spirit. Teach me to anchor my hope in you and to sing praises to your name. I know that you will not fail to fulfill all of your promises to me. Lead me in your paths of righteousness and establish my steps. Send your light and your truth to guide me through this time of doubt. Be my joy and my delight as you set your rainbow in the skies above me. Refresh me now with your sweet songs of mercy and grace. Amen

Perseverance

Knock…*keep knocking.*

Seek… *keep seeking.*

Ask… *keep asking.*

Until you hear a resounding "No" or until the matter is settled in your spirit, you must continue to present your petition to the Lord. Go boldly into His chambers as you plead your case before Him.

Only do not carry the burden of doubt or the weight of worry while you wait for His answer. Ask in great faith believing that your Father has heard and is delivering the answer even now. He will answer your prayer and reveal Himself to you. Settle that in your mind.

Hope *against hopelessness…*

Trust *in His Promises…*

Rest *in His Presence…*

Press in…

Persevere in prayer.

How to Walk by Faith

Scripture Meditation

"Trust in the LORD with all your heart and lean not on your own understanding; in all your ways submit to him, and he will make your paths straight."(Proverbs 3:5-6).

"Thy word is a lamp unto my feet and a light unto my path"(Psalm 119:105).

"…We do not know what to do, but our eyes are on you."(2 Chronicles 20:12).

"He knoweth the way that I take"(Job 23:10).

"The LORD confides in those who fear him; he makes his covenant known to them."(Psalm 25:14).

Musing

As followers of Christ, we walk by faith and not by sight (2 Corinthians 5:7). If it is true that God's Word is a *lamp unto our feet* then it follows that there will be times when we will not be able to see far off into the distance (Psalm 119:105). Scripture does not promise a search light, fog lights, or a beacon that shines for miles ahead. God promises only to light our present path and to illuminate our footsteps as we are taking them.

Those who walk in faith have no worry or fear even when there is no sight or when the way is clouded by a dense and heavy fog. They are able to press on confidently because the One who is leading knows the way (Job 23:10). When things seem impossible faith encourages the weariest of travelers to obediently press on and to trust their way through the obscured path rather than to wait until it is clear. Faith sees things that are unseen and submits to God's plan even when common sense does not see beyond the very next step (Hebrews 11:1). The one who walks in faith can agree with God's plan without fully knowing God's plan. Faith does not need to understand God's ways because faith rests in His indisputable nature. Faith is invested in the facts of God's Word, not in human feelings or emotions. It knows God is present even when the way is cloudy and the path is obscured and believes God to be at work though the evidence of such is not yet revealed. Faith sees God's heart and is confident in His great love.

The disciple who walks in faith walks confidently even when surrounded by uncertainty. She secures her faith by knowing the character of God rather than by knowing things *about* God. The disciple who is grounded in an understanding of God's character and upon the truth of His Word is able to sustain faith even when lacking understanding regarding God's action. Trusting the Father's character allows the faith filled disciple to go forward through fogs in full assurance. By faith she trusts the promises of God's Word because she knows that God cannot lie (Titus 1:2). She can be uncertain of the next step and still be at peace because she is certain of her Father's steadfast character and unconditional love. Her faith enables her to see beyond the clouds and into the heart of her Father as she remembers that everything God does is motivated by His great love. Her faith knows who God is and rests in the assurance that He will never leave or forsake His children.

The disciple who walks by faith knows that God is sovereign and that *if* God is sovereign then He is engineering the events and circumstances of her life. In times of uncertainty, faith will turn to the truth of what God says rather than succumb to the clouded reasoning of fear and fretting (Psalm 37:1). Faith will quell all fear with the assurance that the God who is directing the present path is all knowing and all powerful; therefore nothing is unknown or impossible for Him. The disciple who walks in faith recognizes that each and every breath is orchestrated by her Father. Her life, her path, and each step that she takes are ordained and sustained by Him (2 Corinthians 3:17-18).

The sojourner who travels in faith does not faint because she trusts in the covenant of God and waits for her Father to reveal His will and desires within this current perplexing situation. She will not manipulate or maneuver but by faith she will seek the Father and acknowledge His authority even while uncertain of His strategy in her present struggle. She is totally confident as she waits knowing that God will bring His answers and guide her through His

Holy Spirit. The disciple daughter understands that her Father knows the plans that He has for her and that those plans are intended to bless and not to harm (Jeremiah 29:11). Knowing this truth will enable her to rely upon the power of the Holy Spirit to submit to her Father in the midst of the unknown. She will obediently search out God's Word for guidance and in faith give thanks to Him in advance for the victory that is already hers. Seeing the current situation with eyes of faith will allow her to submit to God's purpose and to acknowledge His plan as the only wise choice for her life.

Any disciple daughter who hears the voice of God calling her to step out in what appears to be the dark of night must trust that as she moves forward in faith the light of His glory will go before her one step at a time and that He will lead her into victory. When Satan seeks to trip up the trusting traveler with doubt and confusion she can keep faith by trusting in the love of her Father. She will be able to trust God beyond her common sense or loss of sight and give thanks in all circumstances (1 Thessalonians 5:18.). This confidence will be possible because her faith knows that through Christ all trials are conquered and that God has specifically met all the needs of the day that waits ahead (Romans 8:37, James 1:17, 1 Corinthians 4:7, 2 Corinthians 12:9). She is already victorious and can thank her Father for her victory even before she enters the battlegrounds.

Heart's Cry

Faithful Father, your Word says that the righteous live by faith. I desire to live in such a way and to be blessed with the knowledge that each step that I take has been ordained by you therefore I am in the center of your perfect plan for my life. Father, there is no better plan. Please teach me your ways as you show me your heart and establish your covenant truth within me. Give me faith. Go with me as my Shepherd and create a grateful and worshipping heart in me. Use the victory that you will give to glorify your name. Amen

Keeping faith by keeping focus

Scripture Meditation

"Moses built an altar and called it The LORD is my Banner (Yahwehnissi). He said," For hands were lifted up to the throne of the LORD. The LORD will be at war against the Amalekites from generation to generation."(Exodus 17:15).

"The Israelites are to set up their tents by divisions, each man in his own camp under his own standard (banner)."(Numbers 1:52).

"But I, when I am lifted up from the earth, will draw all men to myself."(John 12:32).

"Lord, if it is you", Peter replied, "tell me to come to you on the water." "Come," he said. Then Peter got down out of the boat, walked on the water and came toward Jesus. But when he saw the wind, he was afraid and beginning to sink, cried out, "Lord, save me!"(Matthew 14:29-30).

Musing

A banner or a standard is a flag bearing the motto or creed that represents a kingdom, a territory or a political entity. Troops carry their standard into battle and plant their banner within enemy territory after conquering their foes. A flag waving over the tower of a fort or a castle signifies who has dominion there or which power is in residence. Carrying a flag into battle signifies in whose name troops advance and under whose protection they ride.

The American flag is referred to as the "Star-spangled Banner" in our national anthem which was written my Francis Scott Key. The story behind the song is that Key was inspired to write his lyrics upon seeing a large American flag waving over Fort McHenry despite intense bombardment by British troops all during the night. Key knew that the high flying flag waving over the fort at twilight signified the defeat of the enemy and victory for the American defense.

In Exodus chapter 17 we read the account of the attack on Moses and the Israelites by the Amalekites. As the battle raged on in the valley below, Moses, Aaron and Hur watched from their position on a nearby hill. As long as Moses' hands were raised high the Israelites were victorious; but the moment Moses' hands were lowered the Israelites lost ground to their enemy (Exodus 17:11). Moses, Aaron and Hur remained steady all through the night, arms raised, and the Amalekite army was defeated (Exodus 17:13-14). Moses built an altar there and called it: The LORD is my Banner or in Hebrew: *"Yahweh-Nissi"*.

When Moses, Aaron and Hur lifted their hands they lifted their standard or lifted the name of their God high above the battlefield. Moses, Aaron and Hur lifted hands and hearts to God in praise and victory despite growing weary and despite the passing of time. They quickly recognized that as long as Yahweh-Nissi's name was lifted the Israelites were victorious. As long as God's name was the central focus of these three men the Israelites could not be defeated. These three men could not afford to allow their focus to be shifted to the battlefield nor on the strength and number of their enemy. They could not worry about conditions below or shift focus by seeking status reports and casualty updates. A shift in focus away from God to the difficult circumstances of the battlefield would mean certain defeat for the troops doing battle in the name of the LORD. Those high and lifted hands signified victory and brought the defeat of their enemy.

When Peter climbed down out of his boat and first stepped out onto that lake his focus was on Jesus (Matthew 14:23-34). His eyes were looking only to the Lord and in that moment Jesus was greater to Peter than the storm that was rolling in around him. Despite the howls of the wind and the rocking of the vessel, when Peter saw that it was Jesus walking toward them on the water he went to him. Peter trusted Jesus to keep him despite the circumstances, and, he walked on water; something no other human being had done before him.

Then suddenly the disciple lost his footing and began to sink. Nothing within the external set of circumstances changed to cause Peter's sinking situation. The conditions of the lake were not altered after Peter exited the boat. The storm was always present and Peter climbed out of that boat even though it was being tossed about by the intensity of the waves (Matthew 14:24). Peter's faltering steps had nothing to do with the status of the external and everything to do with the status of his faith. In his fear, Peter forgot who had invited him to step out and by whose authority he was walking on the water. He forgot that the one who beckoned him out on to those waves had demonstrated His authority over storms and had once commanded waves to be still. Until Peter lost focus he was accomplishing the impossible because Jesus was empowering him to do so.

Peter lost his focus. He took his eyes off Jesus and in doing so he also lost his faith. It was when Peter allowed the circumstances that surrounded him to steal his attention from the Lord and to shift his focus to himself that he got into trouble. Fear overtook him when his focus shifted from Jesus to the raging storm and the possibility that he might drown. He began to sink when the impossibility of his situation became greater than his faith in the Lord.

The same is true for every disciple of the Lord. It is when we shift our focus away from the Lord and begin to dwell on the difficulty of our circumstances that our steps begin to falter and we succumb to fear. We then sink into despair and disbelief as we convince ourselves that the impossibility of our surroundings is too difficult for even our God to conquer. The shift in focus allows the storm to loom larger as our faith in God grows smaller. It is only when we focus on the truth of the One who has called us and remember by whose authority we engage the enemy that nothing will conquer us or cause us to sink into despair.

Faith requires proper focus rather than ingenuity. We will not make it through the spiritual battlefield upon which we are placed by reasoning ourselves out or by coming up with some creative plan; neither will be succeed by whining and complaining about the difficulty of our circumstances. To claim victory in the face of very real adversity we must believe that God is all powerful, all knowing, ever present and in charge of this current situation. We must know that He loves us and that He is greater than any and every storm that arises (Romans 8:35-39).

Faith is the disciple's assurance of victory because faith is focused on Jesus and Jesus is always the victor (1 John 5:4). He simply cannot fail. God made His Son the conqueror of everything (2 Corinthians 2:14).

Nothing can be too difficult for us because nothing is impossible for Him (Luke 1:37). When we focus on the authority of our Lord and lift up His standard we simply cannot fail. God is present in the praises of His people.

Our victory over flesh and the enemy requires complete focus and dependence upon our God. He is our standard. We carry His name into battle. His name goes before us and assures our victory. Our God is the God above all gods and Jesus' name is the name above all names (Exodus 15:11,Psalm 95:3,Daniel 4:34). At the name of Jesus every knee in every kingdom both in the heavens and on earth is forced to bow and to proclaim Him as sovereign (Philippians 2:9-11).

When God's people lift up hands in praise to His holy name, we recognize that He is our sovereign and we invite His power and authority over our situation. We submit ourselves to the covering of His banner. We raise His name as our standard and claim protection under His dominion. When we to shift our focus away from God and give attention to the storm that rages, the strength of our enemy, or the difficulty of the circumstances in which we find ourselves, we give what is rightfully God's back to the enemy. In doing so, we lower our standard and raise the name of our enemy. Attention is taken from God and given to the tactics of the enemy and to his capabilities. Be assured that when this occurs we will sink into despair and we will lose ground on the battlefield.

As we march forward into battle, let us strengthen our feeble arms and rally around the name of Jesus (Hebrews 12:12). Let us lift high our standard that He might draw all men to Him (John 12:32). Let us glorify the name of the Most High God and proclaim that greater is He who is in us than he who is in the world (1 John 4:4). If God be for us, who can stand against us (Romans 8:31-33)? Let's get out of the boat and focus on the Lord who calls us to come follow Him. In doing so, we can accomplish the impossible.

Heart's Cry

Call to me Lord and empower me to do the impossible in your name. Remind me that I am a daughter of the King of Kings and that I ride into battle under the flag of the God above all gods. Teach me to raise your name in praise over my enemy and to call upon your sovereign power to rescue me and to bring my deliverance. You are my fortress, my strong tower, my redeemer and He who overcame sin and death. Nothing is beyond the range of possibility with you. Amen.

The Father Speaks

"Child,

Listen. Hear me. Draw now to my side.

Lend attention with your ear- open your eyes and see me.

I will speak:

You seek guidance. You ask my help. You seek to know my will.

I have given you a helper; ever present. Rest assured. I have not deserted you.

My will is for you to walk in faith...

Never falter...

Be strong and of good courage...

and hold tight to the promise that I will accomplish what I have set out to do.

You say that you trust me; then rest.

Do not seek to do things on your own.

I have set in motion all things since the foundation of the universe.

I will not now stop merely because obstacles have arisen.

I conquered death and hell on your behalf and gave you the keys to my kingdom.

Why do you come back again and re-ask?

Must I remind you constantly of Who you are?

Where is your birthright?

Have you forgotten the power and majesty of God, your Father?

Stop asking for signs. Move out in faith.

I Am is here. I Am will always be here.

The same God of Abraham and of Isaac is your Father.

The same God who led Moses now waits to lead you.

Commit your path to me.

Rest in the assurance of my faithfulness.

Going On Ahead

Scripture Meditation

"Immediately Jesus made his disciples get into the boat and go on ahead of him to the other side while he dismissed the crowd. After he had dismissed them, He went up on a mountainside by himself to pray. When evening came, he was there alone."(Mathew 14:22+23).

"Who is he that condemns? Christ Jesus, who died- more than that, who was raised to life-, is at the right hand of God and is also interceding for us."(Romans 8:34).

"I pray for them. I am not praying for the world but for those you have given me, for they are yours. All I have is yours and all you have is mine. And glory has come to me through them. I will remain in the world no longer but they are still in the world and I am coming to you. Holy Father, protect them by the power of your name- the name you gave me- so that they may be one."(John 17:9-11).

"My prayer is not that you would take them out of the world but that you protect them from the evil one. They are not of the world, even as I am not of it. Sanctify them by the truth, your word is truth. As you sent me into the world, I have sent them into the world. For them I sanctify myself that they too may be truly sanctified."(John 17:15-19).

"Therefore confess your sins to each other and pray for each other so that you may be healed. The prayer of a righteous man is powerful and effective."(James 5:16).

Musing

On many occasions throughout their training and preparation for ministry with Him, Jesus would send His disciples on ahead while He remained behind. Perhaps He sent them on ahead to see how they would exercise their faith and execute their obedience in His physical absence. Perhaps He needed the time alone to prepare for the ministry or spiritual warfare that awaited His arrival in the next location. Whatever His reason, it is interesting to note what Jesus did after He instructed His disciples to leave Him and to go across the lake alone. Scripture simply states that Jesus prayed (Matthew 14: 24-36).

Scripture does not disclose the contents of Jesus' prayer or share the petitions that He carried to His Father in those moments alone. Perhaps He prayed because he knew that while His disciples were alone on that lake a storm would rise up and their faith would be tested (Matthew 14:24). Maybe, as Jesus watched from the distant shore, He prayed for Peter to have the faith that he would need to answer His call and to walk on those waves to meet Him (Matthew 14:28-30). Jesus might have been praying in advance of all the needs that would be presented from the hundreds of needy people who would be waiting when they arrived on the shore at Gennesaret (Matthew 14:34-36).

We do not know the focus of Jesus' prayer on that day but we do know that He is still praying today. Our Savior and advocate prays for us even as He sends us on ahead (Romans 8:34, John 17:9-11). As He watches from the right-hand side of His Father's throne, Jesus prays that we will be able to see Him walking on the waves of our storms and be willing to trust Him enough to step out of the boat with no shoreline in view. Jesus prays that we will continue to do His work in His absence and dare to be the light shining brightly in the darkness of this sin-sick world. He prays that we will reflect His glory and bring honor to His Father's name (John 14:15-21).

As Jesus prayed that powerful and compassionate prayer recorded in John chapter 17 He released all that was rightfully under His authority to His followers (verse10) and asked that His Father protect us by the power of His name (verse 11). There is no more powerful name in heaven or in earth than the name of The God above all gods and creator of everything- *El Elyon, Elohim* (Hebrews 2:8-10). God bestowed the right to claim the authority carried by that name to Jesus and Jesus was now asking that the Father bequeath that right to us (John 17:12). Jesus asked that we be made safe from the tactics and destructive desires of the evil one and that we be set apart as vessels to be used only for God's holy purposes (verses 15-17). Our Savior offered up Himself as the one who sanctifies us fully (verse 19).

The Shepherd told His Father that He was sending us out in His name just as the Father had sent Him (verse 18). Jesus bought us with His blood and then presented us as fully sanctified to the Father to be used as God wills (Hebrews 2:13,Isaiah 8:18).

As long as God's children are self-sufficient they do not need anything from God. And in their self- sufficiency and pride they will not ask. Prideful people will not pray. Jesus was all sufficient God housed in the flesh of a man. He had all the infinite resources of heaven at His command and yet He practiced the discipline of humble prayer (1 Thessalonians 4:16). One cannot help but wonder what purpose prayer would serve in the life of the human being who had all the power and riches of the kingdom of heaven at His disposal.

Jesus prayed because this action gave Him intimate connection with His Father while He was walking in the flesh. He desired this intimacy each and every moment as He ventured out into this earthly realm to fulfill the will of His father. He received His nourishment, His sustenance, His knowledge and His renewal in prayer. He talked with the Father and His Father talked with Him. It was through this one intimate and direct communication that Jesus discerned both the will and the heart of His Father. Through prayer Jesus' flesh remained rightly related to God and in complete unhindered communion with Him. Through prayer, Jesus released Himself up to the Father and consecrated Himself for the Father's express purpose. In prayer, God's uninhibited life force was enabled in Jesus' flesh and God's perfect will was both discerned and accomplished.

In Jesus' ultimate act of intercession for us; that of becoming the propitiation for our sin, His precious line of direct communication with His Father was severed. Our Savior cried out from the cross under the weight of our sin to ask His Father why He would not now communicate with Him in His hour of greatest need (Matthew 27:45-46). Our sin blocked Jesus from all communication with His Holy Father. It is that same sin and lack of repentance that continues to block human communication with God today.

We refuse to bow our heads and to humble ourselves before our Father in spite of our knowing that Jesus overcame death and sin and that He lives and sits at the right hand of God praying for us. In sinful pride, we refuse to submit to His will or to offer up our bodies- which are already rightfully His to our sovereign God's express will and purpose. In arrogance, we refuse to come in childlike faith to ask for that which Jesus has already bequeathed to us. In doubt and fear, we refuse to go on ahead in faith and in gratitude. We do not trust that Jesus is interceding and that His Father hears and answers His prayers offered on our behalf.

It is when we sincerely believe that Jesus prays for us that we can boldly go on ahead in full assurance of faith and total obedience. There can be nothing that we could possibly require beyond what His prayers and propitiation have already provided. Jesus has commissioned us. He is praying for us. Will we go on ahead?

Heart's Cry

Father God, I ask that you develop a continual, persistent and fervent attitude of prayer in me. Give me a humble heart and a spirit that is totally dependent upon you. As I obediently go on ahead remind me that I am not alone. You have sent your comforter to me and Jesus is interceding on my behalf at your throne. Help me to truly believe that you are my sufficiency. I have no need that you do not see and provide (Jehovah-Jireh). Commission me, Lord, and I will go. Amen.

The Valley of the Shadow of Death

The disciple daughter's fear slowly dissipated as she climbed down out of the fogs and entered into the long and narrow valley before her. While she may have still been nursing cuts and scrapes from her sojourn through the underbrush, rocks, and roots that she had to endure as she crossed through the Wilderness of Want; at least she could now see clearly. She took in a deep breath of air and recalled how at many points during that leg of her journey she had to resort to crawling on her hands and knees through the dense vegetation and snarled thorns that blocked her pathway. It felt good to now stand up straight and to strengthen her feeble knees.

The weary traveler rubbed the back of her stiff neck as she finished the last few steps of the climb down out of that land of clouds and distorted vision. Her leg muscles were sore from spending many hours in a crouched or kneeling position listening for her Shepherd's voice and following the Father's leading. The disciple smiled warmly as she recalled how each night, as the sun began to set, the Father would provide a hiding place within the cleft of those rocks where she could curl up and rest. Then early each morning the Shepherd would lovingly call for her to venture forward on a path that took her deeper still into the rocky terrain that was encircled by clouds and filled with dense fog. Her Father was not the harsh and uncaring Father that she had falsely judged Him to be. He was never distant and though He could have removed any obstacle at any time He allowed them to remain for His good purposes in His daughter's life.

In the land of clouds and fogs the Father had proven His divine wisdom and removed every doubt of His steadfast love. He had taught His daughter to trust even when she did not understand. The Father had restored full confidence in His character and the disciple felt certain that she would never question His sovereignty again. It was amazing how close the enemy had come to her on many occasions. She could hear him prowling among the shadows and just beyond view. At one point she thought she felt his hot breath on her neck and heard his steps closing in on her. The enemy was unable to overtake her even when she was frightened as long as she committed her steps to the Shepherd and stayed close to His side. She was comforted by her Shepherd's staff and knew that He would defend her. She fully trusted Him to fend off any devourer who sought to take her life. Many times along the journey her guide reached out to steady her whenever she lost her footing or became uneasy while crossing the steep and narrowly winding paths. Her Shepherd had also lovingly stretched His body across the opening of her resting place each night and covered her with His cloak. The Shepherd's compassionate actions convinced His devoted disciple that he would willingly lay down his life for her .

Though battered and bruised and bearing the scars of her journey, the pilgrim daughter felt that she had victoriously emerged from her time in the wilderness. She had also come through the fogs and was newly satisfied in her steadfast faith. It was while she was traveling in that wilderness that she openly acknowledged her wants and desires to the Father and slowly let go of those that were not of His will. It was at the end of her journey through The Wilderness of Want that the disciple daughter came to understand that her loving Father was all that she needed and the provider for her every want, desire or secret hope. He had proven to be more than she ever imagined and was able to completely satisfy her longings as nothing and no one ever had.

It was in the fogs that true riches were found in His presence. The Shepherd strengthened her faith, lifted her head and delivered her out of her self- absorbed pity-party. He forgave her of every wandering thought and doubt and was there to guide and to freely impart all things that were good for her well- being. Christ was her provision and her protection. Her spiritual near-sightedness did not blind her totally to the steadfast love of her Father and time spent in the fogs taught her to trust that He was working even though He seemed afar off. Her gentle Shepherd kept her feet from stumbling and stayed closer than a brother as He led her safely out.

Now standing in the center of this deep ravine the disciple could see the steep cliffs that were creating high walls on all sides of her location. She was pressed in on all sides by sheers of granite which had been eroded in some places and bore the ridges and indentations caused by the passage of time. Her feet were standing on a rocky bottom composed of small pieces of rock, pebble and the bones of small animals. She wondered if this place could have possibly been the bed of a once active river or stream flowing down from the mountains and across the steep gradient of those cliff walls. The disciple would never know what this place had once been as the water had long since left and had taken all signs of life and activity with it.

Though the wind was totally blocked by the high walls of the cliffs, the disciple could still hear what sounded like the whistle or moan of a wind blowing across the neck of a bottle. The sound was faintly reminiscent of a baby's cry. These caterwauls and howls seemed to be coming from the mouth of the valley passage and grew louder and more intense as her steps drew her deeper inside the narrow ravine cut into the rock. It was as if the valley itself was crying out in lament or grief. The sound was hollow and haunting and left the disciple solemn and quiet. She imagined the cries coming from the valley to emanate from a reed in the mouthpiece of an instrument being played by the lips of God. The disciple daughter was standing in the middle of the Valley of the Shadow of Death and found herself quietly thinking that this couldn't be happening. She reasoned that she wasn't supposed to be in this place as she had already given up enough. She had proven herself faithful and had made amends for her sinful display of attitudes while traveling though previous territories. Her relationship with her Father had been restored and she was in right standing with the Shepherd. Her guide knew that she was on her way to the King's palaces, not to this place marked by death. Surely it was not now the King's intention for His ambassador to die.

The disciple daughter was frozen in place as the eerie quietness of this valley sent shivers down her spine. She feared that if she entered this place she would soon resemble the gravel and bone fragments lining the long forgotten river bed that formed the valley floor. Surely the Lord did not mean for His beloved daughter to walk through this valley filled with the echoed moans of fear and calls of her enemy. She knew her Savior had already born the guilt of her sin and had paid the full price for her transgressions. She knew His redemptive work in her life and had experienced His mercy and grace. She had submitted to His lordship and was free from all such condemnation. She could not fathom why she was now standing in this place of death or why her guide had brought her here.

The Holy Spirit assured her that this place was not about punishment for sin or about feeling guilty. It was about being willing to identify with the Lord in His crucifixion and about going willingly with Him to die to the control of flesh and self. Her guide explained that it was the Father's desire to perfect her and to impart His sensitivity to the needs of others to her in this place. The Shepherd had demonstrated His great love and willingness to die for her; now she was being asked to become broken bread and crushed feed corn for those whom He loved. The Holy Spirit explained that if she would follow her Shepherd to the Father's holy dwelling place then she must now allow the stripping off of her old habits and behaviors. She must die to the control of her flesh before she could move into the new assignment that awaited her. The guide told her that she would be released to be who her creator intended for her to be and know His power in her life as never before if she would now walk through this Valley of the Shadow of Death.

Sadly, the pilgrim had leaned toward a tendency to become downhearted and distrusting toward the love of the Father who was setting her life course into motion in times past. She had failed to resist the flesh while traversing through the Wilderness of Want and surrendered to emotional outbursts, pity parties, and bouts of indignity. Her heart had grown cold and her passion was overshadowed by her desire for other things. The cuts and bruises that she now bore were the result of stumbling and tripping over her own selfish wants and desires. It was equally true that while crossing the Desert of Transition the sojourner reasoned that her Father was unhappy with her and no longer counted her worthy. She had perceived God's actions as harsh and unjust treatment toward her and as though He was chastising her or giving her a "time out" alone in that place. The longer the journey became the more she worried that her behavior had caused Him to no longer desire to use her or to continue His transforming work within her.

All of that was now behind her. The disciple daughter understood that the Father's delay was due to His great love and that He simply wanted her to rest in Him and to prepare for the trip that He knew still awaited her. Her questions and doubts were gone and her temporarily broken relationship had been reconciled. She felt at peace with her Father as she climbed out of her confusion and trusted the love of her Shepherd as never before. That is why she remained uncertain of the purpose the Father had in leading her to this place of death. Her comforting guide assured her that this valley into which the disciple was now being called to enter would be her final place of equipping and refining. The disciple's great homecoming and journey's ends were awaiting her on the other side. The Holy Spirit had brought her to this place of death to complete her holiness and to remove every shackle or possible stronghold of the enemy that might still remain. This place would remove any remaining aspect of the old sin nature that might prevent her from reflecting the Father's glory.

The Holy Spirit reminded the disciple that her loving Shepherd had endured the shame and agony of the cross for her sake and was now waiting for her to humbly forsake all to walk into death with Him. She failed to remember in her dread and fear that her gentle Shepherd had traveled through this valley before. He had shared the story of His journey here in their times together at home. He was waiting just ahead for her now and would be there to lead the way out to the other side. He had not left her or forsaken her there in that place.

The Holy Spirit also reminded her that growing into spiritual maturity requires the putting away of childish and self-centered things. The disciple now knew that if she would accept the anointing and the mantle of servant hood, and enter into a deeper walk with the Lord, then she must let go of worldly desires and crucify her flesh. She must willingly buddle up her rights and her entitlements and throw them into the fiery furnace of surrender and service. She gulped deeply, rebuked her fear and bravely followed the path of her Savior.

Each fear that the disciple encountered while walking through that Valley of Shadows was the skillfully designed and carefully placed lie of her accuser and her enemy. He toyed with her emotions and tempted her flesh with promises for things of this world. He sought to accuse her and to condemn her. He called out her past mistakes and previous failures as he taunted her with feelings of guilt, unworthiness, and worry. That old spitting snake knew precisely where to strike and how to hit the soft spots and weak places of her soul. But the disciple daughter would not allow the adversary to hinder her progress forward. She held tight to her freedom from condemnation and secured herself in the knowledge of her Father's character. She knew that her Savior had removed her sin far from her and remembered it no more. She was secure in her Father's love.

The disciple grew bold as she neared the altar of The Most High God. There would be no compromise and no tolerance for hesitation. Her old sinful nature had gone into that valley alive and kicking but there could be no future negotiation and no settling for mediocrity. She would no longer be identified with self and would determine to be fully identified with Christ. She had come to do battle and her plea would be "nothing but the blood of Jesus" as she tied her old self to the horns of the altar and held her down.

The disciple was frightened but moved under the covering of her Father's grace and resolved to remain under His sovereign protection. All pretenses, manipulations, cherished idols, and wrong motives would now be put to the sword. Though she trembled, she drew faith by remembering that her Shepherd promised that nothing would separate her from His love. She now placed everything that she had and that she was on the altar before her King's throne. The disciple knew that her redeemer had the right to require her entire life; after all He had purchased her freedom and paid for her righteousness. Even so, she couldn't help but wonder what would remain if she willingly gave up everything and surrendered totally to the final refiner's fire. She questioned who she might be when this was all over. The disciple also wondered if the Father would accept her living sacrifice or if He would burn it up in righteous judgment. She questioned whether her offering could pass the test or if it would be consumed as wood, hay and stubble in the heat of His holiness. She prayed that something beautiful would emerge from this valley of grief and death.

✤ ✤ ✤

Compassionate Conviction and Correction

Scripture Meditation

"Endure hardship as discipline; God is treating you as sons. For what son is not disciplined by his father? If you are not disciplined (and everyone undergoes discipline) then you are illegitimate children and not true sons."(Hebrews 12:7-8).

"Grain must be ground to make bread; so one does not go on threshing it forever. Though he drives the wheels of his threshing cart over it, his horses do not grind it. All this comes from the LORD Almighty, wonderful in counsel and magnificent in wisdom."(Isaiah 28:28-29).

"The Lord is compassionate and gracious; slow to anger, abounding in love. He will not always accuse nor will he harbor his anger forever; he does not treat us as our sins deserve or repay us according to out iniquities. For as high as the heavens are above the earth, so great is his love for those who fear him; as far as the east is form the west, so far has he removed our transgressions from us. As a father has compassion on his children, so the LORD has compassion on those who fear him; for he knows how we are formed, he remembers that we are dust."(Psalm 103:8-14).

Musing

When I was a little girl my mother would tell me that she was punishing me "*for my own good*". She would also assure me as she paddled my little backside that: "this was going to *hurt her more than it hurt me*". Her words were met with great distain and seemed incongruent or oxymoronic to my five year old mind. *If spanking me hurt her more than it hurt me then why in the world did she continue to inflict such pain upon herself?* In **no** way did what she was doing feel good or beneficial to my little bottom (Hebrews 12:11).

As I grew into a teenager, I hated being grounded or losing privileges and often felt that my mother was the meanest woman on the planet. She didn't care if *"all my friends were doing it"*. She didn't care if I would be the laughing stock of the school. Her answer was "no" and that was final. It wasn't until I became the mother of three little girls myself that I began to comprehend the depth of truth that was conveyed by those often recited statements of my mother.

Discipline isn't fun. It is not pleasant for the recipient or for the disciplinarian. It can cause confusion, misunderstanding, hard feelings and a root of bitterness between parents and children if handled incorrectly. As a mother, I have often wished that could simply ignore the improper behavior of my children and have been tempted to turn my head, to look the other way, or to pretend that I did not see the grievous infraction of a family rule. To see my children's disobedience meant interrupting my current occupation and giving of my time to interact with the offending child or to intervene in the situation. Truthfully, it would often have been much easier to throw my hands up in the air and to surrender to the tantrums of a three year old (or a sixteen year old) than to go around on this merry-go round of discipline and correction *one more time*.

I chose to discipline my children because I recognized my responsibility as a loving parent to equip my children to become determined and capable young adults who would be contributing members of the society in which they lived. I realized that if I wanted my daughters' lives to reflect our family's values, and for them to grow into virtuous, God-fearing women; then I had to plough through their anger with me, their storming up the stairs and their waterfall of tears. I had to teach them while they were in the teachable years.

Likewise, discipline is an integral part of the child of God's relationship with their heavenly Father. He administers it through disparate means, delivers it in many forms and allows it to arrive at various seasons and stages of the disciple's development. It is designed to be an instrument of reproofing and refining; and as a means to train us to crucify our flesh through obedient submission to the will of the Lord. Scripture teaches us that going through the process of discipline produces the fruits of righteousness within our spirits and assists in our transformation into His image (Hebrews 12:10-11, 2Corinthians 3:18). Scripture also teaches us that being disciplined is an indication of the Father's love and that everyone whom the LORD adopts as a rightful heir will endure His discipline (Hebrews 12:6-8,Revelation 3:19).

Just as I had an interest in preparing my daughters to live upright and godly lives, so our heavenly Father has a vested interest in our well-being and in seeing that His children reflect His values. He also desires for us to receive the equipping that we will need to endure in our hour of trial , to overcome our enemy in the heat of battle , and to shut the mouth of the lion who seeks to destroy us (Revelation 12:11,1 John 4:4,1 Peter 5:6-8). He is training us to operate in our rightful positions as heirs within His kingdom and teaching us His ways so that we might reflect His character in our daily lives (James 2:5,Philippians 3:10,Psalm 27:11-14,Psalm 103:7). He is using the current opposition, trial, or tribulation to teach us perseverance and to humble us to be used as feed corn for His sheep (Philippians 2:12-16,Isaiah 28:28-29).

The child of God must be careful when being reproofed, or corrected by the Lord, not to allow her spirit to be grieved or to become dismayed and discouraged (Hebrews 12:12-13,Proverbs 3:11-12,Proverbs 15:5). Likewise, she must not allow the enemy to heap condemnation upon her and keep her from returning to the Father to receive His love and forgiveness (John 3:1,John 8:11,Romans 8:1). She can avoid this pitfall by asking that the peace of God guard her heart and prevent the enemy from planting a root of bitterness, or seed of anger, against God for what may seem too harsh or too great a trial at the present moment (Job 5:17-18,Philippians 4:4-9).

When we are disciplined as children of the King of Kings we can nourish our souls by remembering that it is God's love for us that causes Him to take the time to consider us at all; let alone to desire to interact with us as a loving father does (Hebrews 2:6,Psalm 8:1-4).We can also find strength in remembering that God will not always discipline us and thank Him that His discipline is always justice tempered by grace(Psalm 103:9-10).

Rest assured, whom the Lord loves He will discipline and because of His great love for us, our Father will not overlook our sin or allow our improper, immature behavior. We can take comfort in remembering that when He does correct us He will do so in loving kindness and with a Father's heart.

Heart's Cry

Have mercy on me, O God, according to your unfailing love; according to your great compassion blot out my transgressions. Wash away all my iniquity and cleanse me from my sin. Do not cast me from your presence or take your Holy Spirit from me. Restore to me the joy of your salvation and grant me a willing spirit to sustain me. Amen

Neither do I condemn you.

Scripture Meditation

"Then I acknowledged my sin to you and did not cover up my iniquity. I said: "I will confess my transgression to the LORD"- and you forgave the guilt of my sin."(Psalm 32:5).

"Who will bring any charge against those whom God has chosen? It is God who justifies."(Romans 8:33).

"Therefore, there is now no condemnation for those who are in Christ Jesus."(Romans 8:1).

"Then I heard a loud voice in heaven say: Now have come the salvation and the power and the kingdom of our God and the authority of his Christ. For the accuser of our brothers, who accuses them before our God day and night has been hurled down."(Revelation 12:10).

"Jesus straightened up and asked her: "Woman, where are they? Has no one condemned you?" "No one, sir, she said. "Then neither do I condemn you, Jesus declared. "Go now and leave your life of sin."(John 8:10-11).

Musing

The Father has declared that His children are righteous. The gift of His Son, Jesus Christ, justifies us completely (Romans 5:1-2). The Rightful Judge of all mankind does not condemn us because the price for our sin has been paid in full. The declaration of our righteousness was made once and for all by our Great High Priest (Hebrews 7:22-25). Our freedom from condemnation is an established fact that rests upon Christ's death, burial, and resurrection. He conquered sin, hell, and death on our behalf. We are children of the promise. We have been adopted into God's family and have received full privilege as His heirs. These are immutable facts that have been settled in heaven. **It is finished**.

Our enemy, the devil, is referred to in God's Word as the accuser of the brethren (Job 1:7-2:8, Revelation 12). He is a murderer and a liar who has no regard for the truth (John 8:44). This liar dares to present arguments and false accusations before God's throne against God's own beloved children. What is important to recognize within this scenario is that in presenting accusations against God's chosen ones, Satan assumes authority that is not his. He is not equal to the One who sits on the throne of all creation. He is a created being. Likewise, he seeks to bring condemnation upon God's heirs when Scripture clearly states that it is only God who can justify and only God who can condemn (Romans 8). In illegally assuming his role as the false accuser Satan dares to consider himself on equal footing with God and yet he knows that God alone occupies the Great White Throne (Revelation 20:11-15). Making himself equal to The God above all gods is Satan's biggest lie of all.

From the beginning, Satan has sought to usurp God's sovereignty. With his accusations against God's redeemed he now seeks to nullify or cancel out God's purpose in offering redemption, restitution and reconciliation to mankind (John 3:16-21). It is as if Satan has decided that none of that matters. He counts the blood of Jesus as null and void when he brings accusations before the throne of God that have already been accounted for through that blood. He does so in an attempt to disrupt and to damage the relationship between the saints and their Father that was established by the blood sacrifice of Christ.

Satan's accusations and allegations against the redeemed are not aimed at swaying the position or opinion of our Father. He's not that deluded. He knows that the Father is omniscient and therefore is already completely aware of the actions of His children. Nothing is hidden from God's eyes or kept from His knowledge. He does not require a tattle-tale such as Satan to report of the goings on within His universe. Satan also knows that God bases His appraisal of His children upon the vicarious sacrifice of His Son and upon His own promise to forgive us when we repent. God is not the intended audience of Satan's whispered slanders, allegations and lies. He may be hurling these lies in the throne room of God but it is not God that he intends to trip up.

Satan hisses and hurls condemnation and accusations in an attempt to establish strongholds of doubt and shame in the minds and spirits of the children of God. He desires to cripple us and to destroy our confidence in the promises of our Father. He does so by sowing doubt and confusion into the hearts and minds of those who have unconfessed sin in their lives (Genesis 3:1). He utilizes these unconfessed sins as the foundation upon which he builds his strongholds. Satan reasons that if we feel condemned and unworthy then we will hide ourselves away from our Father and shun his fellowship in the same manner that Adam and Eve hid themselves away when they became aware of their fallen condition (Genesis 3:8-9). It is our enemy's desire to separate us from our Father and to cause our pride and arrogance to prevent us from repenting and asking for forgiveness and restoration to rightful standing (1 John 1:5-10). Satan wants us to question the love of our father and base our salvation upon our feelings of worthiness or upon our proper performance rather than upon the facts of God's Word. His greatest hope is that our doubt of the Father's love will eventually lead to feelings of hopelessness, condemnation and guilt. The end result of his plan would be that God's children would be rendered powerless and joyless for as long as they continue to accept his lies. He would then succeed in holding us captive, defeated and powerless because of our broken relationship with our Father. He would also succeed in hurting our Father who desires a rightful relationship with His beloved creation: mankind. Recall that it was God's love that set the entire plan of salvation and redemption into motion. He loved us and sent His Son to die for us while we were still destitute and without hope due to our inherited sin nature (1 John 4:9-10, Romans 5:8).

We can defeat the tactics of our enemy by remembering that when we sin we have an advocate and a High Priest who speaks to the Father on our behalf. Jesus is His name (1 John 2:1-2). Not only is Jesus our intercessor but He is also the atonement for our sin. He is the rightful heir of God and He is our loving Savior. His blood has paid all penalties for all sin including those from the past, the present and the future.

God has sworn a sacred covenant to us as His heirs and has guaranteed it in Jesus' name (Psalm 89:3, Hebrews 6:13-20). We gain victory over our enemy and his cunning lies when we draw near to our Father's throne by the blood of Jesus with the full assurance that we will be forgiven and restored (Hebrews 10:19-22). Satan cannot build a stronghold in the life of the child of God who has no unconfessed sin. When we confess our sin and are restored to right relationship we can then take hold of all of Satan's arguments and allegations against us, bind them up and place them under the authority of our Father's judgment (1Corinthians 10:3-7). God's beloved children can rest in the full assurance that if God does not condemn us, and He does not; then there is no other being in heaven or in earth who can bring a charge against us (Romans 8:33). Jesus has freed us from the power of sin and from the condemnation that sinful acts bring.

Heart's Cry

Father, I am so thankful for the love that you bestowed upon me when you gave up your Son, Jesus, to die. Thank you for freedom from the dominion of sin. Thank you for my righteousness. Thank for making me your heir. I accept your love and come boldly to your throne to confess my sin to you. Do not allow the enemy to drive a wedge between us .Hold me close and convict me of any wrong doing by the leading of your Holy Spirit. I desire to honor you in all that I say and do. Expose the slanderous lies of my enemy and shut the mouth you of my accusers. Amen.

Learning to Pray

Scripture Meditation

"Jesus went out as usual to the Mount of Olives, and his disciples followed him. He withdrew about a stone's throw beyond them, knelt down and prayed."(Luke 22:39,41).

"One day Jesus was praying in a certain place. When he had finished, one of his disciples said to him, "Lord, teach us to pray, just as John taught his disciples."(Luke 11:1).

"Therefore, since we have a great High Priest who has gone through the heavens, Jesus the Son of God, let us hold firmly to the faith that we profess. For we do not have a high priest who is unable to sympathize with our weaknesses, but we have one who has been tempted in every way, just as we are- yet without sin. Let us then approach the throne of grace with confidence so that we may receive mercy and find grace to help in our time of need."(Hebrews 4:14-16).

"In the same way, The Spirit helps us in our weakness. We do not know what we ought to pray for, but the spirit himself intercedes for us with groans that words cannot express. And he who searches our hearts knows the mind of the Spirit, because the Spirit intercedes for the saints in accordance with God's will."(Romans 8:26-27).

Musing

Prayer is learned. It is a habit that must be developed and maintained and a discipline that must become as natural in our daily life as breathing. Just as we cannot live in the physical realm without breathing; we will not survive within the spiritual realm without an effective prayer life; therefore we must get into the habit of seeking our Father in prayer until it becomes an unconscious action. Communicating with the Lord must be the source of our life flow and the motivation for all that we do. John taught his disciples how to pray and the apostle Paul instructed New Testament believers to practice this discipline without ceasing (1 Thessalonians 5:17). Scripture also records the story of Jesus' disciples asking to be instructed in the practice of prayer (Luke, chapter 11). These men had obviously observed their teacher while he was in prayer often as it was His usual routine to withdraw and to spend time alone in meditation and conversation with His Father. They were now requesting to be taught how to follow His example. In response, Jesus gave us an outline that can serve as a guide through the key principles of prayer (Matthew 6:9-13,Luke 11:1-4). If we learn anything from the prayer life of Jesus it is that prayer is essential to anyone seeking to know and to do the will of the Father.

Jesus prayed for His disciples on the night that He was betrayed and led away for crucifixion. He prayed that we would know His father and be one with His Father just as He is one with Him (John 17:3). His prayer granted the followers of Christ the high privilege of communing with the Heavenly Father directly. Access to God through prayer is one of the most precious gifts God has given to mankind; and while God can hear the prayer of an unsaved person, when God's children pray in Jesus name we are promised so much more. We have the assurance that God not only hears us but that He will give us what we ask for when we pray in the name of Jesus (John 14:13-14). Presenting our petitions in Jesus' name identifies us as a family member, authorizes our entrance into the throne room and grants us the approval of the Father.

Jesus' name is the only means by which the redeemed approach our Father in heaven. After His crucifixion and resurrection, Christ went back to His Father's kingdom as the victorious Son of God. Upon doing so He opened up direct access to the throne room of God and positioned Himself as our advocate and only mediator. Jesus also kept His promise not to abandon us after His departure and sent the Holy Spirit to connect our minds and spirits with the mind and spirit of God (John 14:8). This connection occurs each time we pray through Jesus name (John 14:16). Christ's resurrection and subsequent re-establishment of His total authority allows all believers who offer prayers through His name and by the intercession of the Holy Spirit to be in perfect unity with the God-head (Hebrews 4:14-16). Direct communication with the Father, the Son and the Holy Ghost is established each time we engage in prayer through Jesus' name. We become one with the trinity. Being one means that we can communicate with the triune God-head totally uninhibited and unhindered. It also guarantees that God understands our petitions and that we can understand His responses. There can be no language barrier or miscommunication because when we pray in this manner we are able to speak the language of heaven.

The value of a Spirit led and Spirit filled prayer life cannot be overstated. It is through the power of the Holy Spirit that Jesus sent to us after His resurrection and ascension that we become connected with the heavenly Father in such a way that we can now communicate directly with Him and know His will. Submitting to a Spirit led life provides such intimacy with God that we will know His heart and naturally seek His will as foremost in our daily lives. When we are rightly related to God through the indwelling of the Holy Spirit we cannot help but do the will of God because the Holy Spirit dwelling within us is the embodiment of the God-head. If the Holy Spirit is a member of the triune God (and He is) and if He dwells within us (and He does) then **God within us cannot disobey God**. Relying upon the leading of the Holy Spirit when we pray enables us to submit our wants and desires to the will of God and to then pray in unity with the heart of God.

The Holy Spirit also helps in our inability when we do not know how to pray correctly (Romans 8:26-28). He intercedes directly and in accordance with God's will. We are limited in our own understanding of God's plans and purposes when we come before the Father with our prayer requests and intercessions on behalf of others. We cannot know the future or see into the content of a person's heart (Jeremiah 17:10) Sometimes we do not know what to pray because of overwhelming circumstances, or due to our tangled jostle of emotions. At other times we may honestly have no idea of what we need and lack the words to express what it is that we are feeling. There are no such limitations with God. He knows everything and nothing is hidden from His understanding. He holds our future and knows what we will need before we have even presented a request (Matthew 6:8).

When we pray in the name of Jesus and through the Holy Spirit our prayers are not subject to any of the human limitations listed above. We are able to pray the perfect will of God for our lives and for the lives of others. The Holy Spirit goes with us to the Father to help us plead correctly for our wants and needs. Because the Holy Spirit is God, He does know what we need and what is best in any given situation. He knows the mind and heart of God because He is God. When the Holy Spirit is activated within our prayer life He lines up our desires and brings our will into obedience. Remember, *God within us cannot disobey God; neither can He ask for anything that is contrary to God's will or plans.* When we pray through the Holy Spirit, God's will becomes sovereign on the throne of our life and He places all our misdirected, self-interests under His footstool. Praying in the Spirit changes our hearts and our wills to allow us to be more receptive and aware of God's plan (Romans 8:26-28).

Living a Spirit led life in an attitude of prayer keeps us rightly related to God. Submitting to God in prayer aligns our reasoning with that of the Father and allows the mind of Christ to operate within our being (Acts 17:28). Utilizing the name of Jesus when we pray submits our petitions and requests subject to His approval as our mediator and advocate. Praying in His name is giving Him permission to examine our prayers and to then submit them on our behalf in a manner that will be pleasing to the Father. We submit to Jesus' authority when we access the throne using His name. When we establish that position of submission then all of our prayer concerns fall into proper priority and are answered according to God's will. Submitting in this way in prayer acknowledges that we trust God above all and see Him as the source of all that we need. We are confessing that He knows what is best and when is best. Presenting our petitions in Jesus' name and through the Holy Spirit allows us to let God choose for us. We are confessing that we may not know the what or why of our circumstances but we do know that our Father knows all things and we recognize that His grace and His provision are sufficient for us.

After we have presented our petitions in prayer we must then be still and allow the Holy Spirit to speak God's responses to us. We must listen to what He says, be receptive to His instructions and then act upon them. We must choose to allow the Holy Spirit to lead and direct our lives. Though the God-head dwells within us, we are still free to exercise our will in determining whether we go to God in the first place and then again when we decide whether we will obey what He has spoken. Many times our sinful disobedience will lead us to say that we have not heard from God or that we do not know His will when we actually have heard and do know but simply do not wish to obey. At other times we might stubbornly procrastinate to obey in the hopes that God will change His mind and offer us a more pleasant alternative to His original instructions. Take caution, delayed obedience is sin and may prevent God's perfect will and timing in our lives. We must be careful to obey the promptings and nudging of the Holy Spirit if we desire to fulfill the perfect will of God in our lives. Praying in the Holy Spirit will also enable us to wait without anxiety and fear when the immediate and present manifestation of an answer that we seek may not be apparent in the physical realm (Galatians 5:5, Philippians 4:6). The Holy Spirit will remind us that God is listening and moving and working according to His plan, His timing and His will.

A fervent, persistent and continual attitude of prayer flowing from a heart that is humble and totally dependent upon God is essential to victorious Christian living (1 Peter 5:6-10, James 5:13-16). Recognizing this fact, each of us should join with the disciples in their simple request: *"Lord, teach us to pray"*.

Heart's Cry

Lord, teach me to pray and to develop the same attitude that was in Christ Jesus. Make me like-minded and united with you in spirit and in purpose. Teach me not to quench the Holy Spirit that you have provided but to listen to His nudging and to obey His leading. Make your will perfectly clear to me as I yield my members to your service. Amen.

Sacrificial Worship

Scripture Meditation

"Therefore, I urge you, brothers, in view of God's mercy, to offer your bodies as living sacrifices, holy and pleasing to God- this is your spiritual act of worship."(Romans 12:1).

"But the king replied to Araunah, "No, I insist on paying you for it. I will not sacrifice to the LORD my God burnt offerings that cost me nothing."(2 Samuel 24:24).

"But he was pierced for our transgressions, he was crushed for our iniquities; the punishment that brought us peace was upon him, and by his wounds we are healed."(Isaiah 53:5).

"Then Mary took about a pint of pure nard, an expensive perfume; she poured it on Jesus' feet and wiped his feet with her hair. And the house was filled with the fragrance of the perfume."(John 12:3).

Musing

How does one go about the business of being a *living* sacrifice (Romans 12:1-2)? The wording is actually quite confusing and perhaps even oxymoronic in context. A sacrifice is by definition the object being surrendered at the altar of a deity in an effort to appease, or to show reverence, adoration and worship. In the case of the worship of Yahweh in the Old Testament, if an animal was being offered on behalf of a petitioner's sin, the petitioner would lay hands upon the animal and slaughter it (Exodus 6:24-30,Exodus 30:10). The animal's life was being given in exchange for the life of the person bringing the sin offering to God's altar. The animal was killed so that the petitioner might go on living. A sacrifice is dead.

The requirement being made of believers in the New Testament is that we offer ourselves as a *living* sacrifice in an act of worship, adoration, repentance and reverence to our God. (Romans 12:1). We are not being asked to offer up something dead to God. We are not being asked to offer a substitution for our sinful lives. We are being asked to offer up something very much alive and breathing still. Our offering is the surrender to the rights over our own being. God is asking that we bring our lives to His altar and offer up our rights to the control of them even as we keep living.

Mary knew what she was up against as she ventured out of her home that evening. She knew full well that everyone gathered there at the dinner being given in the home of the Pharisee had heard the rumors of her immorality and shameful sexual behavior. She may have even been taunted or shunned and ostracized at one time or another by many of the same religious leaders attending that gathering. Some may have even been counted among those within the circle who had gathered to stone her for her adultery. Mary recognized that she was a fallen woman. But that didn't stop her from pushing her way through the entrance hall uninvited and up to the very front of the room where Jesus was seated. Fear of ridicule, personal embarrassment or the perceived threat of bodily harm was not going to keep her from seizing the opportunity to lavish her admiration and respect on this rabbi who had stopped to notice her and to speak with her as if she were a person with value. Because Jesus had looked beyond Mary's immorality and had moved toward her with grace and compassion; she could now move beyond her sullied reputation and fear of rejection and fall unabashed on His grace. Mary could risk all to pour out her anointing oil on Jesus because Jesus had poured out forgiveness and mercy upon her.

Mary's act of absolute worship and of unabashed adoration was not about her. It was not about the others in the room watching as her spectacle unfolded. It was not about her appearance or even the value of her prized possession. Mary's focus was completely fixed on the object of her love. Nothing else and no one else distracted her from her purpose. Lavishing her love on Jesus was all that mattered to Mary in that moment. Mary allowed herself to become a living sacrifice.

For our lives to be acceptable as living sacrifices the act of living them must be transacted in an attitude of sincere worship. Such an attitude requires that we, just as Mary, surrender ourselves up in an act of total abandon. In essence, we must die to ourselves just as a sacrificial animal would have had to die. We must offer up everything that we are and everything that we have to God when we come into His presence as a living sacrifice. We release everything up to Him because it all rightfully belongs to Him. Every aspect of our life must be stripped bare and spilled out before Him as we fall on our knees at His feet. All was bought by Him in that moment when he stopped to move toward us with great compassion and grace through the sacrifice of His Son: the first living sacrifice.

The offering that we bring in our act of worship must include those things from our life that bring us pride or pleasure as well as those things that cause us pain or shame. All of our living, past and present, must be surrendered at the altar. Nothing about our being is ours to hold any longer. In total surrender to our Lord and our God we must become as that puddle of perfumed oil and be broken, exposed and spilled out completely at His feet. It is at that very moment that the sweet perfume of our unabashed adoration is lifted up to the nostrils of God and becomes a savory offering circulating around His throne (Exodus 30:7). The entire heavenly host gathered to sing praises to the Most High God is surrounded and engulfed in the sweet aroma of our worship.

Just as Mary's perfume penetrated the nostrils and thus the hearts and minds of those men gathered in that room who stood in distain and rebuke of her; when we offer up our brokenness and empty out ourselves in a life of worship, the abundance of God's character can be poured into us and out upon others (John 15:2,2 Corinthians 12:9). When we allow ourselves to be consumed, He is there in the midst of our offering and by His presence we are atoned, made whole and become a sweet aroma. It is at the point of surrendering up ourselves in brokenness that we actualize the precious possession of the person of the Holy Spirit and His power enlivens our earthen vessels. We become the broken alabaster box pouring forth His anointing oil onto others. It is then that the truth of His great love and mercy can be lavished through us and poured out to others.

I dare say that not a single onlooker in that room was left untouched by Mary's act of worship. Every life witnessing her actions was impacted in some way. Likewise, it is through our worship as living sacrifices that others can know God in His fullness and be ushered into His very presence; but we must be willing, as Mary was willing, to give up our most prized possession in total abandon. Whether that prize be our status, position or reputation, accumulated wealth and power, or some deep dark secret that we have carefully folded away and hidden in the recesses of our heart; we must let it go and surrender it up to the lavish grace flowing from the throne of God.

True worship requires the absence of self. Living sacrifices are dead to self and made alive only through Christ (Galatians 2:20). We cannot be concerned for our reputation or for our well-being if we are to be totally broken and surrendered to God. Jesus had no regard for His life or for His well-being as He offered up Himself in total abandon as our living sacrifice. He was stripped naked before all those who watched as His spectacle unfolded. He was beaten, rebuked, spat upon and falsely accused. He did so in an act of total worship to His sovereign Father and in absolute unabashed love for each of us. Mary's alabaster box was broken and all her fear and feelings of unworthiness were shattered. Jesus' body was broken and the dominion of death and hell was shattered. God was well pleased with each of these acts of unabashed worship.

As living sacrifices we should so embrace the act of emptiness that God alone might be able to fill us completely. God offered up His most precious possession, shattered Him against the gates of hell and emptied Him out on the cross that we might be filled with life overflowing and abundant. As disciple daughters called to be living sacrifices we must be willing to offer up all that we are and all that we hold dear and live out our lives in total and absolute worship. Our only reasonable response to God's immeasurable offering is this.

Heart's Cry

Lord, teach me to empty all that is derived of self in total abandon as a living sacrifice to you. Cause me to broken and spilled out before your throne as a savory offering and sweet aroma. May I be broken, contrite, yielded, and humble as I wait for your spirit, your promise and your moving. Use me in the lives of others as you teach me to daily live my life as an act of worship. Amen.

Perfect Love Allows Pain

Scripture Meditation

"In this you greatly rejoice, though now for a little while you may have to suffer grief in all kinds of trials. These have come so that your faith- of greater worth than gold, which perishes even though refined by fire-, may be proved genuine and may result in praise, glory and honor when Jesus Christ is revealed."(1 Peter 1:6-7).

"But he said to me: "My grace is sufficient for you, for my power is made perfect in weakness."(2 Corinthians 12:9a).

"Again, the kingdom of heaven is like a merchant looking for fine pearls. When he found one of great value, he went away and sold everything he had and bought it."(Matthew 13:45-46).

"But we have this treasure in jars of clay to show that this all surpassing power is from God and not from us."(2 Corinthians 4:7).

"Above all, love each other deeply, because love covers a multitude of sins."(1 Peter 4:8).

Musing

The formation of a natural pearl begins when an irritating foreign object is introduced into an unsuspecting mollusk between the mantle and its protective shell. The oyster reacts to the irritant by padding over the substance in an effort to protect its soft and sensitive body. The layers of protection work to distance the oyster's soft body from the irritating intruder and eventually form a pearl. A pearl is literally an uninvited irritant within an oyster's life that has been covered up with layer upon layer of cushion. In the process of pearl making, what was once a difficult and irritating intrusion becomes an object of beauty and of great price.

The Word of God tells us that in this world we will have tribulation (John 16:33). Those who faithfully follow the Lord cannot escape pain and heartache any more than the oyster can leave its shell to avoid the pain and sharpness of its intruder. God's promises to His children do not lift us out of the realm of fleshly living or remove us from the hardships and difficulties of life on this earth. His promises simply give us the grace to endure and the strength to overcome (Romans 8:37).

The good news is that God has not called us to suffer merely for suffering's sake. The Lord has a purpose in all these things. Our Father allows trial and tribulation because He loves us. This is a difficult lesson but God is doing what He knows is best to train us, to equip us and to teach us His ways and His will. Yes, God's perfect love allows pain in the life of His children. It is when we face life's difficult situations believing the depth of God's great love and trusting that His love is true for us in this present set of circumstances that God will sustain us by His grace. In this way, what the enemy meant to destroy us can be used for God's glory and to perfect His plan in our lives (Genesis 50:20, John 19:11).

There will be days when emotional and physical trials will seem too great to bear. God has called us to be obedient and to trust that His grace is sufficient in these difficult and trying times. Our faith is challenged when He does not remove the difficulty that we face as quickly as we would like. At other times we lose heart or fail to understand when He does not choose to remove our "thorn" at all. It is in these times that we can rest assured that our creator has designed us to endure and has given us His grace to cover the sharp intrusions and piercing pain of life. Our part in the process of pearl making is to believe that God loves us and that He is working all things together for our benefit according to His plan (Romans 8:28). If we are going to grow in grace and strengthen our faith, then we are required not only to accept our sharp intruder but to embrace it as part of God's plan. Anything short of seeing God's hand and submitting to His purpose in this present annoyance or difficulty will not suffice.

The oyster does not shrink back from the sharpness of the intrusion. It has no choice but to live with it and to allow it within its environment as it pads it over. Likewise, we must allow God's grace to pad over the offenses, heartaches and trials that we face as we face them. We must not try to escape all of life's trials and tribulations but rather acknowledge them to our Lord in prayer and then surrender them up to His will and purpose. His grace cannot be sufficient unless we believe it to be. He cannot be our very present help in times of trouble unless we allow Him to be (Psalm 46:1). It is when we allow His grace to keep us soft and His strength to be our protection that we remain malleable as the oyster and do not harden ourselves to others or to the Lord. When we rely upon His protection we do not stiffen our spirits and souls in self-protection. It is then that we become the product of His artistry and the reflection of His glory and our trials and tribulations become treasures of great value (1 Peter 1:6-7).

When we develop the discipline to respond to each of life's smallest irritants by immediately bringing them to God we grow in knowledge and in faith and our hardships become a testimony to God's faithfulness and grace. That is because each trial that we face utilizing God's sufficient grace allows us to discover and to draw from the wealth of the treasure that He has deposited into each of our earthly vessels (2 Corinthians 4:7). We learn that we have the love of God, the peace of Jesus, the grace of Christ, the discernment of the Holy Spirit and the mercy of our Father. These precious gifts can be used to transform our natural disposition when facing disappointments, trials and harsh circumstances of life into a thing of beauty to honor our maker and to encourage others. Just as the oyster recognizes that it cannot endure the piercing intrusion of the hard object without incurring great damage; so we must recognize and confess our weakness and imperfection to our Lord. Receiving God's great love while openly confessing our flaws and weakness keeps us humble and allows us to submit to His grace rather than trusting our own ability. It is when God knows our weakness that we can know His strength. It is when our Lord knows our sin that we can know and experience His forgiveness (1 John 1:9). These blessings cannot be ours until we willingly embrace trials and testing as part of our sovereign Father's plan, confess the weakness of our flesh, and then submit to His will because we trust in His great love.

The disciple's strongest shield of defense from spiritual attack in times of vulnerability and distress is total submission to God's will and complete reliance upon His grace. We will not endure otherwise. Victory over our present circumstance will not be ours through any other means. As we fall on God's grace we must anchor our faith in the assurance that Jesus is with us and allow His presence to be our safety and our comfort. Pride, an arrogant spirit, cunning and creative manipulation and righteous indignation will not produce a pearl of great price from a time of trial and testing (James 3:13-18).It is Christ's love alone that covers a multitude of sin. It pads the offenses and sharpness of those people and things that intrude upon our lives (1 Peter 4:8). We must learn to respond to the sharpness of our lives by walking in and exercising the love of God. We overcome the enemy and thwart his attempts to trip us or to lead us into sin when we allow God's grace to cover the irritating life circumstance and to pad our wounded spirits. When we move in grace toward others then He becomes the buffer and the shield in our times of weakness (2 Corinthians 5:14). Our Father can provide the enduring strength needed to protect our tender spots and vulnerabilities from the piercing attacks of the enemy. When we submit to the Father and allow Him to place His grace between the harsh circumstance and our soul and spirit we are then able to avoid fleshly reactions and a hardening of our hearts. Victory is ours when we surrender ourselves to the trial and our will to God's plan rather than wrestle with our emotions. When God's loving children are willing to be vulnerable instead of seeking to protect our rights and feelings, then He can make a cherished pearl out of every difficult and trying situation of life.

Heart's Cry

Father, teach me to call upon your grace in times of sharpness and intruding pain. Be my buffer and my shield from the attacks of the enemy that seek to bruise my spirit and tempt my emotions to a sinful reaction. Teach me to rely upon your wisdom and discernment as I walk this earth and interact with others whom you place in my path. When offended or wounded, do not allow my flesh to rise up within me. Undergird me by your spirit as you stretch my faith and develop a thing of beauty within my life. May I reflect your kingdom and glorify your name. Amen

Nissi or Idols and Asherah Poles?

Scripture Meditation

"The god of this age has blinded the minds of unbelievers so that they cannot see the light of the gospel of the glory of Christ, who is the image of God."(2 Corinthians 4:4).

"If we had forgotten the name of our God or spread out our hands to a foreign god, would not God have discovered it since he knows the secrets of the heart?"(Psalm 44:20-21).

"Break down their altars, smash their sacred stones and cut down their asherah poles. Do not worship any other god, for the LORD, whose name is jealous (Quanna) is a jealous God."(Exodus 34:13-15).

"The weapons we fight with are not the weapons of the world. On the contrary, they have divine power to demolish strong holds."(2 Corinthians 10:4).

"Do not set up any wooden Asherah pole beside the altar you build to the LORD your God, and do not erect a sacred stone for these the LORD your God hates."(Deuteronomy 16:21-22).

Musing

From the day that Adam and Eve chose to yield to sin and to doubt God's word a battle has been raging both here on earth as well as within unseen spiritual realms. At the point of the fall and upon the entrance of sin into the earth, all of God's creation was catapulted onto a battlefield. Nothing was immune from the curse of sin and everything fell subject to God's judgment. All of creation had to choose between sinful rebellion and obedience to the god of this present world, Satan, or obedience and submission to The LORD God (*Yahweh*), the maker of heaven and earth (*Elohim*), the God above all gods (*El Elyon*) for whom there is no equal. It was at this moment that the battle lines were drawn and a war of rebellion against the Lord of Hosts was launched.

Even though Satan and his demons recognize that they are no equal to their creator and that they are defeated foes; they still seek to attack, accuse, humiliate, condemn, guilt, confuse, manipulate, bind, cripple and blind God's people (Matthew 4:3, Mark 1:23-26, Acts 19:14-15, Ephesians 4:8, Revelation 12:10). They snub God's authority and seek illegitimate dominion over His creation (Isaiah 14:13-14). Satan and his fallen angels believe in Jesus and acknowledge that God is indeed God; they simply refuse to bow down to God's sovereignty. They also jealously desire to hinder any pure worship of the one true God and to mislead His followers by seeking to corrupt their walk with sin (Psalm 74:4, 2 Corinthians 4:4).

The LORD instructed the Children of Israel not to place any other gods before Him (Exodus 20:3). He also warned against building altars and erecting standards of strange gods in the company of His standards and altars (Deuteronomy 16:21-22). Such compromise and acceptance for pagan religion was not to be tolerated. The God above all gods would not share His territory with strange gods nor allow their altars and asherah poles to be erected near His sacred habitat. God ordered that all the altars and asherah poles of strange gods were to be cut down, smashed and burned (Deuteronomy 12:3). The Israelites were also commanded not to approach their God with the same form or worship that the pagans offered (Deuteronomy 12:4).

At the point of salvation, the Holy Spirit seals the believer and raises the standard of God's kingdom over the throne of their will to indicate that God is in rightful dominion and residence there. Every disciple is bought with a price by Christ at the point of conversion and then been set apart for a very special purpose for the glory of the one true God alone. Our bodies become His temples (1 Corinthians 6:19). We are sacred and set apart unto Him (Ephesians 2:10, 1 Peter 2:9). Things devoted unto the Lord are for the specific use of the Lord and are not be used for any other purpose. The sacred cannot be used to perform the duties of the profane. As the vessels of the Lord we are His consecrated possessions. We must be careful not to allow tolerance for anything that is contrary to the teaching of the Word and the prompting of the Holy Spirit. We must not offer up our members in service to any deity other than the Lord God Almighty.

Idolatry is the worship of false gods and would include anything that usurps the rightful authority of God or that is placed on the throne of a Christian's life. Just as the Holy Spirit raises a standard or plants a flag to stake a claim to a territory or a being; our enemy raises his standards (*Asherah poles*) as an indication of his occupancy or claim on a person, place or thing. Remember, Satan cannot claim any territory within the believer that has not been previously surrendered up to him. He cannot enter where he is not invited. Believers often give our enemy an opportunity to enter, and to establish a stronghold through our unsubmissive spirits, rebellious thoughts, and the desire to be vindicated or proven right. He gains ground into our lives when we yield to the sins of the flesh and give them a place in our thoughts, actions or attitudes (Psalm 7:14-16,James 1:15). Satan is searching for any little soft spot or weak area within the believer's spirit that he can penetrate and begin to worm through. That is why it is important that we confess our sin and repent before the Lord for every wrong thought, attitude and action. Each sin that remains hidden and unconfessed can quickly become an entry way for the enemy to get a foothold and to plant his standard.

God's ambassadors are commanded to demolish all strongholds and to destroy the work of our enemy (Mark 13:34,John 14:12,1 Peter 5:8,1 John 3:8). Our assignment must include the capture and destruction of the enemy's standards that might be staked within our own spirits and emotions. The most subtle or covert altars are often those dedicated to the protection of attitudes and emotions such as resentment, unforgiveness, arrogance, vengeance and selfish pride. Disciples must be careful that they do not allow altars dedicated to such things as worldliness, self-promotion, retaliation, or the need for approval, and the protection of a good reputation to remain standing.

The Father has provided His ambassadors with mighty weapons that are effective for tearing down idols, demolishing strongholds and destroying asherah poles. These are primarily a working knowledge of the Word of God, and willing submission to the power of the Holy Spirit (2 Corinthians

10:3-7,Galatians 5:16-26,Hebrews 4:12). Anything counterfeit, or counter to the will of God, will not be allowed to rule in a disciple whose spirit has been armed with the truth of God's Word. Light has no fellowship with darkness and the disciple who walks in the spirit cannot fulfill the lusts of the flesh (Galatians 5:16,Ephesians 5:11,1 John 1:5). The Spirit of God abiding within the believer cannot disobey God.

Idols that sometimes remain unidentified within the disciple's life include those things that are looked to for fulfillment or satisfaction. These could include the desires for wealth, for a position of status, for church membership, and for relationships with family or friends. Anything that takes primary position within the disciple's thought life or imagination, their financial resources, and time or affection can become an idol. Even a desire for ministry, and the rituals and routines of Christian living; such a Bible reading, daily devotional time and church attendance, can become idols if a disciple is seeking fulfillment or to gain a sense of worth and approval through them. The disciple of the Lord must be careful that recognition for service in God's name does not become more important than spending time in the Lord's presence and actually seeking His face.

The disciple who wishes to avoid idol worship must immediately bring every thought captive to the Lord and humbly repent before the Father. This humility before the Lord will empower us to resist the temptations and cajoles of the enemy (2 Corinthians 10:5,James 4:7-10). We must also crucify our flesh and our self-motivated desires if we are to keep our enemy from staking a claim in our lives (Colossians 3:5-10). Taking our stand and boldly proclaiming the truth of the cross of Christ defeats the attempts of the enemy to bind us and to make us ineffective warriors.

As the spiritual battle rages on today, Jesus is our *Jehovah-Nissi*; our standard and our rallying point (Exodus 17:14-16). He is to be the disciple's focus on the battlefield and the assurance of our victory. Jesus told us that if He would be lifted up that He would draw all men to Him (John 12:23). Ambassadors of God's kingdom must lift the name of Jesus higher than any other and seek to glorify the Father above all the earth (Psalm 8:1,57:11). Jesus' name is above all names and all authority is rightly His. It was given to Him by His Father after Christ's resurrection (Matthew 28:18,Ephesians 1:22). It is in this powerful name and under His rightful authority that the ambassador of God claims victory and marches into the enemy's territory. In that mighty name the ambassadors of God's kingdom can tear down our enemy's asherah poles and put him on the defensive. We can march into his territory and stake our claim through Jesus Christ our standard (Genesis 22:17, Isaiah 37:26, 41:13-15).

Heart's Cry

Oh Father God, you are God alone. There is none other than you. I desire to live as your chosen vessel; holy and set apart for your service. Teach me to discern every spirit and to acknowledge your sovereign headship over the throne of my life as I submit my body as a living sacrifice to you. Expose any standards or asherah poles that the enemy may have erected and help me to tear down every altar of idolatry against you. Bring to my mind any sin from which I need to repent. I lift the name of Jesus as my standard and proclaim that He is Lord of my life. Amen.

Soul's Desire

My Soul desire is to know you, Lord…
to be lifted from this natural plain into your Holy presence…
to be transfixed by your glory and to gaze up into your eyes,
to fall down at your throne and to kiss your feet.

Oh for a span of time measured in eternity to praise you
and to exalt your name!
It would not be time enough.

For you are altogether lovely
and altogether beautiful.
My Maker
My Master
My Redeemer
My Lord.

Less means everything

Scripture Meditation

"…You still lack one thing. Sell everything you have and give to the poor, and you will have treasure in heaven. Then come follow me. When he heard this, he became very sad, because he was a man of great wealth."(Luke 18:22-23).

"He must become greater; I must become less."(John 3:30).

"I have been crucified with Christ and I no longer live, but Christ lives in me. The life I live in the body, I live by faith in the Son of God, who loved me and gave himself for me."(Galatians 2:20).

"Therefore whomever humbles himself like this child is the greatest in the kingdom of heaven."(Matthew 18:4).

"The Lord alone led him; no foreign god was with him."(Deuteronomy 32:12).

Musing

Exactly what was Jesus asking of the wealthy young man when instructing him that he must first give away everything that he owned if he desired to inherit eternal life (Luke 18:22-23)? The requirement must have been interpreted as too great by the young man because Scripture tells us that hearing the words that Jesus spoke left him speechless and that the young ruler walked away from Jesus' offer in somber silence without further expression. He did not scoff or try to ridicule Jesus for demanding too high a price. He did not argue or seek to barter. He simply turned around and left the Lord's presence. For whatever reason, the young man simply could not, or would not, meet Jesus on His terms.

Perhaps the rich young ruler was saddened when we went away because he recognized that giving away everything meant losing all his material goods or creature comforts along with his status, prestige and clout. The young men knew that if he met the terms that were being exacted he would no longer live or conduct business in the usual manner. His name would not carry the same recognition or response and his life would be forever changed. Following Christ would mean leaving a life of title and position to become someone without prestige or a place of honor.

Perhaps the young ruler recognized the authority in the Lord's voice as Jesus addressed him. He may have often spoken to his own house servants and employees with this same matter of fact tone. Following this rabbi whose words seemed to carry such influence and strength would require that the young man surrender his will to the teacher's instructions and yield to the master's commands. Entering a life of submission and humility would not have come easily for a young man who took pride in his religious piety and who was accustomed to having dominance or authority (Luke 18:21). Perhaps the young ruler did not want to relinquish control of his life and surrender his future to the hands of this itinerant teacher.

Scripture indicates that this young man came to Jesus in the hopes of transacting business. He had come to inquire about inheriting (earning) eternal life not about entering into a life of indentured servitude (Luke 18:18). Perhaps, on some level, the young man felt that his strict adherence to the law had earned him merit or had already placed him ahead of the crowd in terms of deserving the prize that he now sought. What he was really asking from the Lord was for him to consider the pious life that the young man had led up to this point and then to simply point out where he needed to make corrections or what he had yet to do if he were to obtain his goal. Perhaps his speechless reaction was the result of the astonishing requirement that he become a pauper in his present life to earn eternal life. He came to Jesus considering eternal life as an easily obtainable goal or one that was reasonably within his reach and went away in grief as he was unable to pay the price required.

What does it mean for the disciple of Christ when the voice of the Lord calls out requiring that we surrender everything to follow Him? A life of discipleship demands that Christ occupy the position of priority in the disciple's life. His will must be first and foremost in our thinking, desires, and in our daily occupations. The totally devoted disciple cannot have regard for resources, for reputation, or for the preservation of person or property. She cannot be concerned with the daily cares of her life but must cast all her cares upon her Maker and trust His provision to be sufficient for her needs. The one who chooses to follow the Lord cannot allow anything to be of greater value or concern than total obedience to the will of the Father. The disciple's will and energy must be totally yielded to the master's designs.

The eternal life that Jesus imparts cannot be generated through living a life of piety or religiosity. It does not originate from earthly sources. It cannot be purchased but flows freely from the throne of God. Eternal life is a gift that if given to anyone who humbly recognizes Christ as the source from which she must draw and the strength upon which she must rely. Acquiring eternal life requires coming to God with the humility of a child. The decision to become His disciple demands the willing death to the life that was once led (Matthew 18:4, Galatians 2:20). The will, goals, and desires of the self must become less and less significant in each and every aspect of the disciple's life if she is to be imbued with the fullness of life that is God's alone to give (John 3:30).

The words that Jesus speaks to us today are no less demanding or straight forward than the words that He spoke to that rich young ruler. What Jesus requires of His disciples is still everything. Becoming His disciple will require that we give away every self-designed dream, hope, aspiration, and vision to surrender our futures completely without hesitation or doubt. It has never been God's will that His children be anything other than totally surrendered to His will and totally secured by His love. As God's children, we must learn to rely upon His strength and His wisdom rather than to place our trust in our own self-righteousness, affinities, knowledge, and talents. Following Christ requires that we remove anything that is false, pretentious, prideful, or derived of the flesh in order to become His simple, trusting, and obedient child (Luke 18:17). If we are going to be His disciples then we must be crucified to our old life and made alive in Him. We must die that Christ might live (John 3:30).

We can choose to accept the terms that Jesus offers and to agree upon the price of discipleship or we can walk away grieved by what seems too high a cost. Those who choose to follow Christ agree to lay their lives at His feet and to transact all living according to His sovereign will. We cannot take up the cross without denying the flesh. We cannot follow Christ without forsaking all others. We cannot be His until we are no longer our own (Mark 8:34).

Heart's Cry

Father, bring me to a point of selflessness. Empty out all that is derived of my old sinful nature that I might be a vessel filled by your Holy Spirit and used according to your will and purpose. Help me Lord as I renounce my own agenda and submit my will totally to your control and sovereignty. My desire is to be totally devoted to you as your daughter. I surrender the throne of my life to you and recognize you as God alone. Remove all performance orientation from my thinking as I become more aware of your grace, mercy and great love for me. You are my everything. Amen.

The Choice for Humility

Scripture Meditation

"When I was a child, I talked like a child; I thought like a child, I reasoned like a child. When I became a man, I put childish ways behind me."(1 Corinthians 13:11).

"Humble yourselves before the Lord, and he will lift you up."(James 4:10).

"Do nothing out of selfish ambition or vain conceit, but in humility consider others better than yourselves."(Philippians 2:3).

"So he got up from the meal, took off his outer clothing, and wrapped a towel around his waist. After that, he poured water into a basin and began to wash his disciples' feet, drying them with the towel that was wrapped around him."(John 13:4-5).

Jesus said, "Father, forgive them, for they do not know what they are doing." And they divided up his clothes by casting lots."(Luke 23:34).

"Carry each other's burdens, and in this way you will fulfill the law of Christ."(Galatians 6:2).

Musing

Many people misunderstand the Bible's teaching on humility and misinterpret what God's Word actually means when we are instructed to humble ourselves and to live out our lives in humility (Philippians 2:3). Being humble does not mean being a *wimp* or becoming a doormat; to be humble is not the same as to grovel, to whine, or to have no opinion. Likewise humility cannot be equated to simply possessing a mild-mannered or passive disposition. True humility does not derive from a position of weakness or passivity at all but actually requires great discipline, determination and a focused personal strength. Living a life of Biblical humility should never be seen as an act of diminishment. Living according to this model actually increases one's strength and it is when someone is willing to humble themselves that they become most strong in the Lord. True humility allows the disciple to break free from any earthly entanglements and stumbling blocks. Approaching Biblical humility with the understanding that being a discipline of Christ actually increases our power will allow us to view humility as a positive in our lives rather than as a negative.

Godly humility is derived from being comfortable with who we are in Christ and feeling good about our identity with Him. It requires that God's will and His kingdom receive preeminence within our life. Spiritual maturity is required by anyone determined to live a life of humility because living in such a manner demands that the concerns of others be placed above the desires of the self. Humility also requires that one respond to the actions and attitudes of others with a servant's heart and attitude (1 Corinthians 13:11). This *others-centered* perspective will only be possible in the disciple who understands the great value of all that is acquired when exchanging feelings of self-worth and self-esteem for an identity in Christ. It is when the disciple is willing to humble herself, and to base her identity in Christ rather than in her own personal achievements or acquisitions, that she is able to rest her reputation and validation in His hands. It is then that the child of God can willingly lay down all that she is and possesses in service to others without regard for return (John 15:12-13).

When the disciple's identity is in Christ there is no need to be defensive, to be correct, or to be noticed, and rewarded by others. Identity in Christ allows the disciple to be able to esteem others above themselves. She can surrender the right to defense and to being offended, and avoid being manipulated or needing to manipulate others in order to get selfish needs met(Galatians 2:20). The disciple's ego is no longer central when she is evaluating herself looking through the heavenly Father's eyes and utilizing His standards rather than some worldly measure. Grace towards those who offend, falsely judge, ridicule, or accuse will be motivated by the recognition of the disciple's own sinfulness and need for Christ's redeeming grace. This grace will compel the disciple to get her eyes off herself and to dedicate her life in service to the one from Whom, for Whom, and through Whom all things exist and are sustained (1 Cor. 8:6,Col.1:16-20).

A new identity in Christ means that one's heritage is no longer traced through the line of Adam. The follower of Christ is now a fully recognized member of God's family and is adopted into the line of Christ. God has forgiven each of His children for personal sin- past, present and future. Through Christ Jesus, He has also delivered them from the heredity of the sin nature. That is to say, God has changed our identity status from being members of sinful humanity to being full members of His sinless, heavenly kingdom. We are heirs to the righteousness of Christ rather than heirs of the sin nature of Adam. Through Christ we have received abundant life (John 10:10). Through Christ, every spiritual blessing has been freely given to us as the children of God. Our eternal destiny is established in heaven (Ephesians 1:3,Phil. 3:20-21).This is the truly awesome status of those who place their identity in Christ. We must never down play or dilute the absolute marvel of this truth. Through the grace of God, those who claim identity with Christ are adopted heirs of the kingdom of God (1 John 3:1). Hallelujah!

As heirs to God's kingdom, the attitude that the disciple displays should be the very same as the one that Jesus bore (Philippians 2:5-8). Walking in Biblical humility requires balancing an awareness of the value of our newly established identity in Christ Jesus with a call to a life of service and an attitude of esteeming others above oneself. The disciple must avoid an attitude of selfish pride or arrogance but shouldn't deny the gifts or talents that God has bestowed but neither should she minimize the unsearchable richness of Christ's grace (Ephesians 3:8). Walking in humility requires that the disciple be cautiously aware that the old fleshly nature can lead her astray and cause her to fall into the same trap that the disciples fell into if she begins to seek honor for those things that belong to the Father. She must remember that these gifts and talents are bestowed to accomplish the work of the Father and for the glory of our Savior. They do not belong to her or originate from within her flesh. They are gifts given to her by her Father. It would be absurd for anyone to desire credit or recognition for a gift that was given to them by someone else. True humility is an attitude of submission to the will of Christ, recognition of

His great grace, and a sincere desire that all glory and honor go to Him because He alone is worthy. Acquiring such humility will require that the disciple seek the things of Christ Jesus rather than fleshly desires for recognition, reward or approval (Philippians 2:21).

Each disciple daughter should remember that we must choose to serve in humility before the Lord. The priority desire of our wills should be to be a vessel fit for God's use and dedicated to His service alone. This attitude is accomplished by following Christ's example and by examining His attitude and behavior. The Son of God practiced a level of humility that allowed Him to wash the dirty feet of His disciples, to eat with sinners and to visit the homes of despised tax collectors. Jesus was able to serve others and to walk in total humility because He was completely secure in His identity with His Father. He had no need for a false front or to preserve His image or status which freed Him to respond to criticism and to ridicule without defensiveness, condemnation or shame. The humility of Jesus placed Him in correct relationship with His Father and with the others whom He was called to serve. It was Christ's humility that enabled him to obey the will of His Father in total freedom and without fear.

The disciple's freedom to enact the absolute uninhibited will of God begins with a "**C.H.O.I.C.E.**" She must *choose humble obedience instead of choosing ego or emotional reactions.* She must place the will of the Father above the motivations of the "**S.E.L.F.**" (*Selfish, emotions and lusts of the flesh*). Doing so will require that the disciple crucify the flesh and consider others above themselves (Galatians 2:20,Colossians 1:18). When the kingdom of God has preeminence in the life of the disciple she will be empowered to respond to unfair treatment without being overcome by such emotions as unforgiveness, bitterness or anger. She will have no need to seek vengeance or revenge (Ephesians 4:31-32). Choosing to respond in humility will empower the disciple daughter to hold her tongue when falsely accused and to forgive others because she understands the debt she owes for Christ's forgiveness toward her. Her humility will enable her to rise above all the bondage of former fleshly emotional strongholds and to activate the power of God's Holy Spirit. Moving in the fruit of God's spirit will prevent the disciple from reacting from a position of pride or self-centeredness.

The disciple's decision to walk in a Christ identity and to be motivated by humility places her in a position of power because such an identity establishes freedom from sin and deliverance from the bondage of selfish desires. Choosing to exercise Biblical humility will enable God to take the throne of the disciple's life as He transforms her from glory to glory (2 Corinthians 3:18). All self-willed, immature flesh will give way to God's sovereignty as His love is freed to flow, to touch and to change the lives of others.

Heart's Cry

Oh Father God, have access to my life and to my will by the power of your Holy Spirit. Make me a channel of your love and blessing to others. Teach me to crucify my ego and self-centered immaturity as I seek to walk in Christ-centered humility with you. Bless the work of my hands to increase your kingdom rather than to inflate my ego. Help me to live my life seeking your agenda and doing your will rather than seeking to serve my own purpose. I acknowledge your lordship and the preeminence of your will in my life. Pour out through me into the lives of those whom you have called me to serve and help me to fulfill your purpose. Amen.

Finding Identity by denying Self

Scripture Meditation

"When the Lord saw that he had gone over to look, God called to him from within the bush, "Moses! Moses!" And Moses said, "Here I am"." (Exodus 3:4).

"But Moses said to God, "Who am I, that I should go to Pharaoh and bring the Israelites out of Egypt? And God said, I will be with you… "(Exodus 3:11-12a).

"God said to Moses, "I am who I am. This is what you are to say to the Israelites: I AM has sent me to you."(Exodus 3:14).

"Then Jesus said to his disciples," If anyone would come after me, he must deny himself and take up his cross and follow me. For whoever wants to save his life will lose it, but whoever loses his life for me will find it."(Matthew 16:24-25).

Musing

Moses was not a young man when God called to him. He was well educated and experienced. He had a wife and children. He had taken up residence with a Midian priest, married the man's daughter and started a family and a new life within a foreign land (Exodus 2:11-22). He lived there as a shepherd tending his father in law's flocks, according to Scripture, for a *long period* before God called to him from the burning bush (Exodus 3:23). Moses was established in a new community and had left behind the history of his past. It is also probable that he was fully aware of the stories of God's provision and protection from his infancy given that his own mother was appointed his nursemaid by Pharaoh's daughter (Exodus 2:8). Moses knew the story of his rescue from the waters of the Nile and of God's divine placement of him within the palace walls. The very name given to him by Pharaoh's daughter at the time of his weaning meant that she had drawn him out of the water (Exodus 2:10). Despite Moses' knowledge of God's intervention and presence in his life when God shared His plan to appoint Moses as the deliverer of His people, Moses seemed to suffer from a sudden attack of identity crisis and "low self-esteem". The "Here I am" he uttered at the burning bush quickly shifted to "Who am I?". Moses questioned God's wisdom in choosing him and tried to excuse himself as unqualified (Exodus 3:11).

The ailment from which Moses actually suffered in that moment appears to be more a case of cowardice than of identity crisis and insecurity. There was actually a no better suited man to plead the cause of the Hebrew people before the throne of Egypt than Moses. Moses had connections and was known within the royal courts. For forty years he ate the food of Pharaoh's table, slept under the protection of Pharaoh's guard, and enjoyed all the fineries that any member of the royal household enjoyed. Moses lived in the laps of luxury while his own relatives lived as the slaves of Egypt and endured a life of hard labor under their difficult taskmasters. All of this was God's design and purpose for Moses from the beginning. He had not landed in Pharaoh's household by accident. God knew who Moses was when He called him. His Maker had been operating toward him in providential grace all of his life. Each of the events of Moses' life was in preparation for God's present purpose.

Moses' sudden attack of insecurity could have been motivated by more than the fear of failing God. His desire to avoid Egypt could have been about saving face as well as his own skin. Moses hadn't always acted as a coward in the face of injustice in times past; neither had he spared the use of violence. When Moses was forty he killed an Egyptian who was beating a Hebrew and consequently had to flee from the comfort and provisions of his palace home. He avoided being put on trial as a murderer and being lawfully executed by fleeing to the desert of Midian. He met his father in law, Jethro, due to his bravery in coming to the rescue of shepherdesses who were in distress while trying to water their father's sheep (Exodus 2:12,16).

It could be that Moses' trepidation to return to Pharaoh's courts was due to the fact that he was well known rather than because he was an unknown. Moses knew that he had a sullied reputation. He was a criminal and a wanted man. Perhaps he was afraid of returning to Egypt and of consequently losing his life. Perhaps Moses was worried that the members of Pharaoh's court would not take him seriously; given that he had grown up among them. His concern might have been that when he presented himself as the deliverer of the Israeli people, he would be received with the same level of disrespect that was shown him by the Hebrews who witnessed Moses commit murder (Exodus 2:12-14). Those folks in Egypt knew who Moses was and what crimes were buried in his past. He hadn't made restitution under the law and his debt was still unpaid. How was a criminal in the eyes of the law going to now pass himself off as the hope of the Hebrew people now enslaved in Egypt? We may never know the true motivation behind Moses' objections to the Lord's call but Scripture does tell us how God responded to those objections.

It is interesting to notice God's response upon hearing Moses' pleas of insecurity and insistence in his lack of qualification. He did not rebut Moses' protests by recounting Moses' history to him or try to reassure him of his qualifications. God did not extol Moses' virtues or begin to list all of Moses' talents and abilities. He didn't remind Moses of his education, pedigree or of skillset. He didn't pull out a genealogy or chart his lineage or try to bolster Moses' faith by recounting God's faithfulness in delivering him from infant death. God didn't remind Moses that it was His mighty hand that had provided that Hebrew child with a home behind palace walls. He did not seek to make Moses feel special or try to convince him that he was the best man for the job. God did not seek to build Moses' self-awareness or to bolster his emotional security; He didn't even tell Moses not to worry about his past sin or reassure him that everyone had forgotten his criminal history. Though any of these tactics might have been employed by a human agent seeking to encourage someone to accept a commission; Scripture doesn't indicate that God utilized any of them.

God did not rely upon the lineage, skillset or resume of Moses to substantiate that choosing him was the right decision. God's guarantee of Moses' success was founded upon and secured in the fact that God was sending him and going with him (Exodus 3:12,14). God was calling Moses' to a totally God-centered and God sustained identity, and to a way of living that was God-focused rather than self-aware. Nothing in Moses' person or his past was the motivating factor of importance that God submitted as His reason for selecting Moses. God simply told Moses that He was with him and He was sending him. That fact was enough in God's eyes. God had a plan and chose Moses to fulfill it. God would accomplish His plan because He was God; not because Moses was Moses. Moses was about to learn the difference between *doing for* God and *being used by* God.

True discipleship requires more than devoting one's talents, skills and abilities to a social cause or to a person. Being qualified for ministry is not based upon having developed a healthy self-esteem or being self-actualized. Being called by the Lord is not about the one who is called but rather about the One who is initiating the calling. True discipleship requires self-crucifixion not self-sufficiency. It is realizing that nothing good is born of the flesh and that every good and perfect gift comes from the Father above (James 1:17). The disciple does not enable God; it is God who enables the disciple.

True discipleship is the total surrender of the self to a life of absolute obedience to the will of God without giving place to insecurity, hesitation or doubt. It is a life in which we relinquish our control, our will and our self-sufficiency to make Christ the center of our being. Living out God's plan and accomplishing His purpose in our lives requires total surrender to God's sovereign rule and a shift away from self-conscious living to God-consciousness. When God called Moses He called him to the life of a servant. At that burning bush God told Moses to take off his shoes in recognition of God's superiority and as a sign of Moses' submission and servitude (Exodus 3:5). As God's servant, Moses relinquished all rights to a "say-so", vote or right of objection. His life was no longer his own.

The life of a disciple is one of *initiation* rather than *imitation*. It is one of self-denial rather than self-actualization. A disciple's life is one that is Spirit empowered rather than self-sufficient. We cannot merit God's willingness to use us by legalistically copying Christ or by doing our best to do as Christ did. All of our attempts at righteousness are as filthy rags and our flesh will never be qualified outside of the blood of Christ Jesus. (Isaiah 64:6-9, 2 Corinthians 5:21).When we become God's ambassadors we are asked to die to ourselves and to allow Christ's life to be released within us. When we submit to God's life lived in us, our lives are limitless and without impossibility because the One who is empowering our being is eternal and beyond all possibility. He is omnipotent and omniscient. We are fully able to accomplish what God desires of us only when we are in a unified relationship with Him and are allowing His Spirit to be the source of all power, wisdom, assurance and capability. We do this when we move away from a self- supported and self- identified life and into a Christ identity (Romans 6:13-22,Galatians 2:20). When we become a vessel that is emptied of self and filled with God's power we are able to live and move under His Spirit's volition and our source is the life of Christ living in us (Acts 17:28,2 Corinthians 4:7-9).

As a living sacrifice we rely totally upon the Spirit of the living God to raise us up after we have crucified our flesh and been buried with Christ. Disciples are not called to aspire to be better human beings, or to act more like Christ; we are called to allow Christ to live through us and thus transform us into a closer likeness of Him (2 Corinthians 3:17-18). As living sacrifices, we are dead to self-rights, self-preservation and the protection of reputation. We become a willing slave to the grace and mercy of Christ Jesus (Romans 12:1-2). The disciple of the Lord is no longer self-motivated or self-focused because the self is dead. The life now being lived is being activated and empowered by God's Spirit (Galatians 2:20). God is able to dwell in and to resurrect that which we offered up to Him. This is how our righteousness is made possible and how our transformation into His image is transacted (Romans 3:22-24,Romans 5:1). It is by His power and has nothing to do with our capabilities or accomplishments. We do not get selected to be ambassadors of God by getting in touch with our inner strength or by proving our hidden talents. These displays do not impress our Father. He knows who we are when He calls us. More importantly, God knows who HE is. He asks us to die to our self-reliance and to trust Him to be our sufficiency.

The weary disciple must never anticipate that God will bolster our frail self-image or build up our self-esteem in order to convince us of why we are of value to His service (Romans 3:9-19). God did not do that for Moses and He will not do it for us. Our identity is to be found in Christ alone and not through any merit of our own (John 17:20-25). Our value is that we are

God's children and as such are unconditionally and dearly loved (1 John 3:1). Our qualification is His calling rather than our deeds (Colossians 1:9-10). The disciple must choose to follow the Lord as a transaction of the will and not as the response of human talents or emotions (Joshua 24:15).

Heart's Cry

Sovereign God, I desire to live a life that is empowered and enabled through the indwelling presence of your Holy Spirit living in me. Demolish all the arguments of my fleshly doubt and rationalizations and move me beyond all the limitations of my sinful inheritance as I surrender to your sovereign rule and begin the process of transformation and regeneration. Oh Lord, be the source of my life and being. Help me to find my identity in you and to know my value as your precious daughter. Remind me that nothing is impossible for me because you are with me and you are sending me. Amen.

The Home Coming

As the disciple daughter exited the mountain range that housed the Valley of the Shadow of Death her path opened up to a grassy meadow full of fruit trees that gracefully bowed and danced beside babbling brooks. They were heavy with fruit and the perfume of their blossoms filled the air. She could hear children laughing and the sounds of a distant heralding trumpet. Standing tall on the horizon were the towers of the King's palace. His banners were unfurled indicating that the king was in residence. At last the weary traveler had reached her journey's end. She had emerged victorious and was now being ushered straight ahead to the dwelling place of her Father. Her guide told her that the Father had left His throne room upon hearing of her arrival and was coming out to meet her. She was assured that the King would be preparing a banqueting feast in her honor and would present a robe and a ring bearing the insignia of His kingdom to His faithful daughter. This ring would signify that all the riches of heaven were rightly her's.

The leisurely and more restful stroll across the meadow lands of the King allowed the disciple daughter time to reflect upon her travels and the exploits of her wilderness experience. She now realized that much of the trauma; heartache and loneliness that she endured were of her own invention. The loneliness and confusion along with her extended time meandering away from home and far from the presence of her Father were the direct results of her responses to the trials and tribulations that she faced as she journeyed. As she looked back at her journal entries the disciple daughter realized that she had spent far too much of her traveling time in bitterness, doubt, complaint and discontent. She had lost her focus many times in the muddled fogs, had failed to listen for her Shepherd's voice in the wilderness, and had failed to relinquish her grasp on all the secret things that she had coveted or desired. The disciple had been reluctant to destroy all of the altars of idols that she had rebelliously erected in her heart and now realized that her passage through the Valley of the Shadow of Death had taken longer than she had hoped because of her self-motivated idolatry. Many of the strongholds of the enemy that she had allowed in her life had deep foundations. These took time to dismantle and to totally uproot and overthrow. It also took more time than necessary for her to bundle up all her rights to her self and to her dreams and to throw them into the refining fires that burned in front of the throne of God.

The disciple daughter could also see the places while traveling through the Desert of Transition where she had taken matters into her own hands and had allowed her pride to carry her headlong off the path that the Shepherd had loving placed before her. She defied His sovereign rule, and stubbornly ignored His pleas to *be still*, or to wait, while He put things in proper order. It was because she did not wait on the Lord's perfect timing and did not rest when He directed that she became weary in well doing and yielded to the temptation of impatience, impertinence and self-pity. Her sojourn through that sand was much harder than it could have been had she simply heeded the Shepherd's instructions and stayed on His ordained paths. It is a wonder that she did not fall into more pits of despair than she did. The disciple daughter was so thankful for the grace of the Lord. Each time that she slipped He would soon come along and lovingly pull her out of the mire. He would set her feet back up on the more stable sand and start back down the appointed back as He beckoned her to follow.

The disciple daughter learned too late that she had not always trusted her Father's promise to meet her needs. She also failed to focus her attention on His presence rather than coveting what was not yet hers or wallowing in self-centered absorption. Perhaps if she had exercised childlike faith and been more trusting then her Father's purpose could have been realized much more quickly. She felt certain that there would have been far less roots and snarled branches along her path and therefore less to trip her up. She might have walked out of the wilderness and into her Father's presence much sooner and been given her newly inherited territory earlier. The disciple daughter was heartbroken over her rebellion and grieved to think that she had been so short-sighted. Her Father had always been so gracious and loving towards her. It saddened her to think that she could have ever questioned His provision or His perfect plan.

The wearied though much wiser pilgrim now understood the purpose in her time away. Her loving Father simply desired to call her to a time of solitude and intimacy before leading her into widened territory, greater work and increased responsibility within His kingdom. Each of her times of trial and of testing was designed to draw her closer to Him and to encourage her to seek His face. The Father wanted His beloved daughter to use this time of solitude to learn His ways and to become more aware of His character and nature. He wanted to strengthen their relationship and had hoped that despite her times of confusion and doubt she could trust His love and anchor her faith in His promises to never leave her or forsake her. The Father wanted His daughter to continue to look to Him to supply her every need. The disciple daughter now understand that if she had done as the Father had hoped then her time in the Wilderness of Want would have been much shorter and her paths would have been wider and more clearly lit.

The pages of her now complete travel journal carefully detailed the passage through the varied sets of circumstances into which her call to obedience had led. Retrospectively leafing through the notes she had written helped her realize that the Father had worked His purpose in her times in the desert, the wilderness, the valley and even while cloistered away in those suffocating fogs. What the enemy had tried to use for the destruction of her faith and her relationship with her Father, God had used for her deliverance from self and for the transforming restoration of her soul, body and mind (2 Corinthians 3:18). She also now understood the need to go away with the Lord more often and to seek the Shepherd's guidance with each step of her daily walk. She vowed to consecrate her future life for the Lord's service and to offer herself up to be used as the

Father's willing vessel. The disciple daughter loved her Father with a new found passion and sought to fulfill His purpose with greater zeal. Her time away had not been in vain. It had actually been a rich and glorious experience. The things that she had learned while traveling through each trial and tribulation would never be forgotten and she emerged from her travels transformed and revitalized.

The triumphant traveler had arrived safely at the king's dwelling place at last. As she rounded the corner of the path leading to His chambers, she could see that her Father had left His throne room and was standing on the path directly in front of her with outstretched and extended arms. A great crowd of saints had gathered and were waiting to greet her. Her loving and faithful Shepherd was standing at the right side of the Father and appeared to have a gift of new royal robes draped across His arm. She stepped up her pace and hurried along the pathway that ended at her Shepherd's feet. She bowed down before Him and tearfully lifted her voice to praise her Savior for His sustaining grace, redeeming love, and enduring patience. All of heaven's host sweetly joined in her chorus of worship and praise.

As the disciple daughter tearfully knelt before her Father at this glorious and final homecoming she wanted more than anything to hear Him say that she had successfully finished the assignment that He had given her. She longed for the Father to see that though she had often failed Him, she had actively sought to glorify His name and to live a life that reflected His character. The whole assembly waited in silence before the King in anticipation of His words to His daughter. The Father reached out in compassion to the disciple daughter and lovingly embraced her as He cupped her tearstained face in His hands. He smiled down and welcomed His daughter home and into His presence.

The King and His daughter chatted intimately as they walked uninterrupted within the kingdom gardens. The disciple had lost all measure of time basking in His presence and listening to His secret thoughts and dreams. The King then led His newly appointed ambassador out into the open fields of His kingdom and exposed the vast territory that He was now entrusting to her keeping. The fields were white with harvest but there was much to be done before bringing it into the Father's storehouses. The King had established His daughter in a new place of ministry and had opened up wide doors to opportunities for ministry. As she surveyed the vastness of this expanded territory and all the opportunities that it presented, the disciple daughter realized that she could not complete all the required work alone. She asked the Father if He might provide others who would come alongside her in her ministry. The Father smiled and assured His daughter that her time in the desert and the wilderness without the company of other saints was ended. This new territory in which He was placing her was inhabited with likeminded believers and other members of the family of God with whom she could share her journey. These other disciples would encourage her, love her, and help her to deepen her understanding of God's character. Interaction with these kindred people of God's kingdom would challenge her walk and sharpen her character. Together these believers would learn to trust the same Savior, to honor the same God, and to wait in the hope of the same returning King. They would learn to love each other now in the anticipation of an eternity spent together in heaven.

The king's daughter had completed her time of refinement and was ready to be a channel of living water and blessing in the lives of others. Her time of travel had taught her how to become broken bread and poured out wine in the lives of those whom the Lord had called her to love and to serve in His name. She prayed that her words would be a healing ointment and a cleansing balm for the wounded and hurting who would cross her path, and asked that she might always remember to respond in grace towards others, just as Christ had been so gracious to her. The disciple daughter recognized that it was the Shepherd's love towards her during her time of wandering that now compelled her to love those whom He entrusted to her keeping.

While it was true that the disciple daughter would never forget her time away with her beloved; she was ready, at least for now, to call this newly inherited territory home. She had found her way back to the Body of Christ and to fellowship and ministry after her time of solitude and refining. She would be a solitary traveler no longer. The disciple daughter was now ready to share all that she had learned and to offer up her gifting to the benefit and growth of all those to whom she would now be joined. She was totally yielded and surrendered to a life of service that promised to be dynamic, living, breathing and forward moving. She would faithfully accomplish all that her Father placed before her until she heard His voice quietly beckoning her to come away with Him once again.

This is Holy Ground

Scripture Meditation

"The commander of the LORD's army replied: "Take off your sandals, for the place where you are standing is holy." And Joshua did so."(Joshua 5:15).

"When the LORD saw that he had gone over to look, God called to him from within the bush, "Moses! Moses!" And Moses said, "Here I am." God said, "Take off your sandals, for the place where you are standing is holy ground."(Exodus 3:4-5).

"However, the Most High does not live in houses made by men. As the prophet says: "Heaven is my throne, and the earth is my footstool. What kind of house will you build for me?" says the LORD. Or where will my resting place be? Has not my hand made all these things?"(Acts 7:49-50).

"Jesus replied: "If anyone loves me, he will obey my teaching. My Father will love him, and we will make our home with him."(John 14:23).

"You also, like living stones are being built into a spiritual house to be a holy priesthood offering spiritual sacrifices acceptable to God through Jesus Christ."(1 Peter 2:5).

"Do you not know that your body is a temple of the Holy Spirit, who is in you, whom you have received from God? You are not your own; you were bought with a price. Therefore honor God with your body."(1 Corinthians 6:19-20).

Musing

As the Children of Israel traveled through the wilderness they carried the Ark of the Covenant with them to serve as a reminder of God's presence wherever they went. Prior to the establishment of the covenant through the giving of the law to Moses, God would lead His people through the wilderness with a pillar of cloud by day and by a column of fire at night (Exodus 13:20-22). An established physical dwelling place for God did not exist until the Tabernacle was later constructed according to a pattern that God gave to Moses (Exodus 25:1-27:20). This tabernacle remained the centralized location of worship for the people of Israel until King Solomon erected his magnificent temple. He ordered it filled with the Ark of the Covenant as well as with all the treasures that had been consecrated to God by his father, David. Scripture recounts that after the priests placed the Ark of the Covenant within the temple and withdrew that the cloud of the LORD filled the sanctuary (1 Kings 8:6-12). Afterward, this temple was forever dedicated as holy ground. It was consecrated and set apart as a place for God's people to come into His presence and to beseech His attention. It was the place to hear His words and to carry out His commands.

Earlier in Scripture, we read that Moses encountered another place that was consecrated as holy ground unto the LORD (Exodus 3:4-5). This sacred ground was not surrounded by an ornate or elaborate edifice. God did not meet Moses in a gold covered, silk draped sanctuary. The Most High God chose to meet Moses on the far side of the desert near Mount Horeb (Exodus 3:1). He came to Moses on an ordinary work day, in the midst of the wilderness, and spoke to him while abiding within an everyday scrub brush. God proclaimed this ground upon which Moses was standing as holy unto Him ("*Kodesh*").

Joshua, the man who took up the mantle for leading God's people after the death of Moses, found his holy ground as he was kneeling before the commander of the LORD's army while encamped within the plains of Gilgal (Joshua 5:10-15). He was contemplating the impending battle at Jericho when God called out to him just as He had previously called to Moses. In both instances these men were instructed to remove their sandals because the place upon which they stood was holy unto their God (*Kodesh*).

We can see from the examples listed above that a number of things with a wide range of properties or esthetics were considered sacred or holy unto our God. The temple was holy as were the tabernacle, an ordinary bush and a location near the Jordan River. It was not some particular property possessed by the items listed or their locations within God's creation that qualified them as holy unto the Lord. Holiness has nothing to do with the characteristics, properties or components of the item being labeled as such. The dirt in which the desert scrub brush grew wasn't unique or imbued by God with special gifts or powers. The temple and the tabernacle were each made from ordinary materials and were not fabricated using extraordinary, other worldly materials. The spot near the Jordan River where the commander of the LORD's army stood wasn't a sacred location due to its position upon the globe. The label *holy* is not derived from an item's uniqueness. Scripture clearly indicates that ordinary people, places and things become *holy* unto our LORD.

Scripture in the Old Testament contains a detailed outline of the garments that God instructed were to be included in the wardrobe of the High Priest (Exodus 28). These verses describe the priest as being clothed from head to toe in the finest linens and with the most precious jewels. His headpiece and breastplate were coated in gold. He also wore a turban, called a *crown of mitre* that had a gold plate attached to its front with blue cords. The words "Holiness unto the LORD" were engraved on that plate which rested continually on the priest's forehead (Exodus 28:36-38). To qualify as a priest a person had to be anointed for the service of God. Every member of the priesthood was consecrated and set apart specifically for the LORD's use and to tend to the business of The Most High. This consecration and anointing was engraved clearly on their forehead for all to see. These men were ordinary descendants from the lineage of Aaron who were chosen to perform the extraordinary task of carrying out God's work among His chosen people. These ordinary men became holy unto God when they were set apart for God and meant for His specific use or occupancy alone. Their consecration meant that they were no longer a part of the mundane or of the profane though they found their origins in ordinary, mundane, earthly beginnings. The same is true of the scrub brush, of the tabernacle and of the temple. Holiness is not about the item or the place but rather all about the God who consecrates, inhabits and uses it for His purposes.

Christ is present among His people today in a special way. He has promised to be with us always, even to the end of the age (Matthew 18:20;28:20). The New Testament teaches that the Holy Spirit indwells Christ's disciples and that God makes His dwelling place within those who obey His teaching (John 14:23). We who believe in Christ are God's spiritual house. We make up the living stones of the temple of God (1 Corinthians 6:19-20,1 Peter 2:5). God dwells in us! Thus, we are holy ground because wherever God dwells is holy. We are His holy dwelling place just as the tabernacle and Solomon's beautiful temple were His holy abode. We are holy because the God who has chosen us and who indwells us is holy (1 Peter 1:13-16).

The New Testament also teaches that all Christians are part of the royal priesthood who serve under Jesus, our High Priest (Heb. 2:17,3:1;1 Peter 2:5-9;Rev. 1:6;5:10;20:6). We wear our consecration on our foreheads just as the priests of the Old Testament did. We bear the mind of Christ as our engraved identification to transform us beyond the thinking of this ordinary world and to prevent our thoughts and emotions from being held captive by former things (Romans 12:2,2 Corinthians 10:5). Our flesh is ruled by God and put under the subjection of the Holy Spirit who writes His laws upon our hearts and instructs us in His ways. We are filled with the presence of The Most High and marked as God's holy vessels (2 Corinthians 4:7). Our bodies, now His sacred vessels, are available, sanctified and set-apart, for the use of the Lord. God can do whatever He pleases with us.

We are Holy unto God. We are His burning bush, His temple treasure, His implement of worship, His royal priest, His living sacrifice, and His abiding place. Praise His holy name!

Heart's Cry

Father God, thank you that through your grace you have sanctified me and made me holy unto you. Lead me by the direction of your Holy Spirit as I desire to be a temple vessel used by you to proclaim truth and to set your people free. Speak through me as you did through the burning bush. Abide in me as your holy tabernacle and anoint me as your priest. I present myself as your living sacrifice today. Amen.

A New Thing

Scripture Meditation

"Forget the former things; do not dwell on the past. See, I am doing a new thing! Now it springs up; do you not perceive it? I am making a way in the desert and streams in the wasteland."(Isaiah 43:18+19).

"Oh LORD, you are my God; I will exalt you and praise your name, for in your perfect faithfulness you have done marvelous things, things planned long ago."(Isaiah 25:1).

"Therefore, if anyone is in Christ, he is a new creation, the old is gone, the new is come!"(2 Corinthians 5:17).

"Not that I have already obtained all this, or have already been made perfect, but I press on to take hold of that for which Christ Jesus took hold of me. Brothers, I do not consider myself yet to have taken hold of it But one thing I do: Forgetting what is behind and straining toward what is ahead, I press on toward the goal to win the prize for which God has called me heavenward in Christ Jesus"(Philippians 3:12-15).

"Come now let us reason together, says the LORD. "Though your sins are like scarlet, they shall be as white as snow; though they are red as crimson, they shall be like wool. IF you are willing and obedient, you will eat the best from the land but if you resist and rebel you will be devoured but the sword". For the mouth of the LORD has spoken."(Isaiah 1:18-20).

Musing

It is exciting when I consider that the God who created everything that presently exists and ever existed in times past utilizing absolutely nothing but His sheer will and power is in the process of (re)creating you and me. He first made us alive in Christ *(rebirth)*. He forgave our sins and paid our debt through the gift of His Son, Jesus (*restitution, redemption*). His act of redemption also *restored* us to right relationship with God (*reconciliation*). He then deposited the Holy Spirit within us to begin the process of *regeneration* (1 Corinthians 2:12). If we are identified with Christ then we are new creations and all things are made new in us through the washing of His blood and the regenerating works of the Holy Spirit (2 Corinthians 5:17-21,2 Corinthians 4:16,).

Because we vicariously died with Christ, we now have the capability to live in a manner that pleases God the Father. We have the power, given to us by the God who created everything, to become all that He is able to create within us. The range of possibility would be an infinite and never ending list as nothing is impossible for God or beyond the scope of His imagination. The grace of God made us a new creation at the point of salvation and is continually making us a new creation in our present circumstances and daily walk (Colossians 2:7,1 Corinthians 2:10,Romans 5: 10-17). This transformation into all that God desires for us to be is an on-going process. We are new now and become newer still with every passing moment that we spend in His presence and surrendered to His sovereignty. Moment by moment we are changed from glory to greater glory still. Hallelujah!

The key that unlocks this process of regeneration and renewal is ours to take and to use. It is one of the keys of the kingdom that Christ gave to us at the point of our adoption as rightful heirs of God (Matthew 16:19, Ephesians 1:5-11). The authority to unlock the door that ushers us into kingdom living is part of our rightful inheritance but is operated only when we are willing and obedient (Galatians 3:29). All the power of God's kingdom is at our disposal as long as we choose to walk within His authority and following His will (1 Peter 2:9,1 Thessalonians 5:13,Romans1:7,Colossians 1:12). When God's children honor His will they walk in newness of life, have power over the dominion of sin, and are empowered to obey God (Romans 6:4,Romans 6:14,Philippians 2:13).

If, however, God's people choose to resist and to rebel against God's will then they cannot enjoy God's best, be guarded by His peace or be guided by His spirit (Isaiah 1:18-20,Philippians 4:7,Psalm 48:14). Our fellowship with God is broken by our sin and the Holy Spirit's work within us is halted until we repent, seek His forgiveness and submit to His authority once again. Our free will decision to either obey or disobey God determines our relationship with Him as well as the blessings from which we benefit (Romans 8:22-25,28,Isaiah 30:1,Isaiah 43:1-7). We can determine to have our own way or we can determine to be identified with Christ. We can choose life or we can choose death and we will reap the outcome of those decisions in our daily living (Deuteronomy 30:15,Galatians 6:7). The process of renewal and regeneration requires that we decide to leave our former life behind and choose to keep our flesh in perfect union and subjection to Him. This is what frees the Holy Spirit to work within us and through us.

It is hard to conceptualize what life could be for the disciple who would be willing to let all the creative power of Almighty God rule in her heart and soul in complete uninhibited authority. It is just as difficult to imagine the outcome in the life of the disciple who was totally open to the Holy Spirit's transformative and regenerative work. Such marvels are unfathomable to the finite mind. Imagine what would be the result in your life, disciple daughter, if you would let go of your ideas about how your life should be and simply desire to become all that God wants you to be. There could be no limitation on a life that was totally released to the LORD as His handiwork (Ephesians 2:8-10). The life that was lived in uninhibited and intimate relationship with the God who has unlimited power, all-knowing wisdom, incessant love, and complete creative will would be unlimited. Mighty works could be accomplished through the vessel who was willing to overflow with God's regenerative and reconciling ministry into the lives of others.

If our spiritual life has become stale and our life in Christ has lost all joy and enthusiasm, if our walk with the Shepherd has become an endless cycle of meaningless motions and powerless ritual; then perhaps it is because we have failed to seek God. Perhaps we have failed to ask Him to show us His glory and to give us His power in our daily walk. We may have ceased to expect the unexpected and the miraculous to occur in our midst. Our staleness may be due to our disobedient, stubborn or ungrateful attitudes which have caused us to stop asking God to glorify Himself in us and to do new and wonderful things in and through us. If God is not dwelling richly in our lives with total and uninhibited sovereignty and undisturbed dominion then we must confess it, accept His forgiveness, be restored unto Him, and press on to obtain that which He has for us. It is then that our lives can become limitless, bountiful, victorious, and blessed beyond our capacity (Psalm 23:5,Malachi 3:10).

Those who are willing to submit their lives to God can see and know the kingdom of heaven while still living within their fleshly dwelling (Deuteronomy 29:29,Daniel 2:22,Luke 17:21,John 3:3). They can also realistically choose not to yield to sin (1 John 3:9, Romans 6:7-14). They will become more than conquerors as their daily living is imbued with the supernatural power of God (Acts 1:8,John 14:12). As God's children we can know and do the will of God because we have the mind of Christ. We are partakers of Christ's divine nature and we are sealed by the Holy Spirit (1 Corinthians 2:16,2 Peter 1:4,Ephesians 1:13). Therefore, we are overcomers and become indestructible instruments of Christ's righteousness (I John 5:4-5,1 Peter 1:23,Romans 6:13). We have access to the fruits of His Spirit to monitor and to control our fleshly emotions (Galatians 5:22-23). We are enlightened and encouraged because we are confident that He will finish that which He has began in us (Ephesians 1:18,2 Thessalonians 5:16-17,Philippians 1:6). We are assured that all things **will** work together for good in our lives and that we will see God someday face to face (Romans 8:28,Matthew 5:8,1 John 3:2-3).

God desires to do a new thing in each of His disciples. He desires to move through us to accomplish the plans that He determined for us long ago. He longs to make paths in the desert for us, and to be an artesian spring of living water pouring forth refreshment as we cross through the tangled and rocky wilderness of our lives. Our God can open up our graves, move over us in compassion and grace, loose the grave cloths that bind us, and bring our old dry bones back to life (Ezekiel 37:3). But first we must present ourselves out of our own free will as living sacrifices and willing vessels sanctified totally unto Him (Romans 12:1-2,1 Thessalonians 5:23). God will do the absolutely impossible and miraculous things that have never been seen before in the life of the saint who is willing to believe in Him as the Almighty. He will impart all that He is into the one who will risk everything to partake of His goodness. Oh to dare to imagine the possibility of a life that is totally surrendered to the touch of the Almighty.

✠ ✠ ✠

Cinthia W. Pratt

Heart's Cry

Father God, I present myself as a living sacrifice and a willing vessel. I ask that the Holy Spirit prepare me with a new vision, a new joy and a new desire to be totally surrendered to you. Do a new thing in me and through me, LORD. Renew my vision, my strength and my commitment. Regenerate, refresh and revive my spirit. Continue your good work in me as you breathe newness of life into these dry bones and lead me through this desert to your springs of living water. Amen

But there are Giants!

Scripture Meditation

"They gave Moses this account: "We went into the land to which you sent us, and it does flow with milk and honey! BUT the people who live there are powerful, and the cities are fortified and large" (27)… "But the men who had gone up with him said: "We can't attack those people; they are stronger than we are."(31) "We seemed like grasshoppers in our own eyes, and we looked the same to them" (33) (Numbers 13:27,31,33).

"You, dear Children, are from God and have overcome them, because the one who is in you is greater than the one who is in the world."(1 John 4:4).

"In addition to all this, take up the shield of faith, with which you can extinguish all the flaming arrows of the evil one."(Ephesians 6:16).

"The Lord gave them rest on every side, just as He had sworn to their forefathers. Not one of their enemies withstood them; the Lord handed all their enemies over to them. Not one of all the Lord's good promises to the house of Israel failed; every one was fulfilled."(Joshua 21:44-45).

Musing

Why should we be surprised when we encounter obstacles after stepping out in faith to obey God or to actualize a vision that He has shared with us? When we hear the voice of the Lord commanding us forward we must not expect that all will be easy or trouble free. Too often, as disciples, we wait for the path to be made easy or for the obstacles to be cleared before beginning to walk out our territory or to claim our rightful inheritance. We forget that it was often God's pattern throughout His Word is to give His children a promise or a vision and then to lead them into a time of preparation and of warring against great obstacles before they received all that He had spoken. Living a life of faith often required being willing to engage in real battle. David fought Goliath. Joseph was thrown into the pit. Moses wandered in the wilderness. Paul wrote most of the New Testament from behind prison walls.

Scripture reminds us that even while Jesus was in the very same boat with His disciples they encountered a real and terrible storm on the lake (Mark 4:35-41). Please don't miss the irony that this storm rose up right after Jesus had spent that afternoon speaking to the crowd that had gathered around that lake on the subject of faith. He shared three separate parables on this topic while these very same now fearful shipmates were in ear shot. The disciples heard Jesus teach on faith right before they loaded the boat to cross over to the other side (Mark 4:1-34). Jesus was with them but His presence did not prevent the storm winds from blowing.

Caleb and his men saw the giants that inhabited the land that God had promised the Children of Israel. When the spies saw the mighty strength of those unlawful inhabitants of their promised land they become as grasshoppers in their own eyes (Numbers 13:33). They gave up. These men assumed defeat before they even started to fight. They quickly forgot in whose name they came (1 Samuel 30:8,Zechariah 4:6). They failed to recall God's faithfulness to them in the past. They did not remember that nothing was impossible for the person who places their faith in the God of Abraham, Isaac and Jacob because nothing is too difficult for God (Jeremiah 32:27,Matthew 17:20). These mighty men of valor forgot that the battle belongs to the Lord (Exodus 14:13-14,Deuteronomy 31:6,2 Chronicles 20:15).

Do not be surprised, disciple daughter, when there are giants blocking the path as you move forward to claim what God has promised. When you see them you can choose to throw up your hands and to throw in the towel or you can choose to believe all that God has said and to stake your claim. You can choose to stand in faith, fully armored as you lift up the sword of the Lord and shout your victory or you can retreat in defeat before you even attempt to fight.

The victorious disciples of the Lord are those who recognize that *Jehovah Sabboath*, the Mighty Warrior, the Commander in Chief of all the heavenly realms, is our King. He rides out before us and accompanies us into battle (2 Chronicles 20:15-24). He throws lightening to expose the enemy and clashes the thunder as cymbals announcing His coming. All of His creation is full of the signs of His awesome power. He can engage all of that power to battle on His child's behalf. There is no equal to our God and none can defeat Him.

The child of God who is presently engaged in spiritual battle can maintain faith and be encouraged to keep fighting when she understands how it is that she is seeing the giants and great obstacles that presently block her path. They are visible to her because the Lord has exposed them. He has uncovered the hidden obstacles and strongmen that seek to prevent her from receiving her promised inheritance. They are no longer hidden to her. The battlefield has been completely disclosed and the disciple knows what it is that she is up against. Because of the discernment of the Holy Spirit that is made available to her, this warrior is not walking into a situation blindsided or unaware. The Father does not show His warriors the enemy that we face to frighten us but rather that we might study them, know their tactics, their routines and their vulnerabilities and then stand and see the victory of the Lord (Luke 4: 18-19,1Peter 5:6-8,1 John 2:24-28). God reveals giants and then conquers them and enslaves them to do His bidding (Joshua23:3-11).

As ambassadors of a heavenly kingdom we are in a real battle and on a real battlefield. We get wounded and hurt and often bear the scars of battle in our emotions and spirits. The Lord does provide us with armor, weapons and the assurance of victory but we must develop the discipline and the skills to practice faith and to engage in battle with the enemy (Ephesians 6:10-18). We can speak with authority to the giants and other obstacles that we encounter only when we are in right relationship with the Lord. The ability to discern His timing and His will come only through a relationship with Him (Matthew 16:19,Romans 8:37). The disciple warrior obtains the victory when she is bold in prayer and has faith to believe that whatever she prays in faith has already granted by her Father (Mark 11:24). She can stand fast and lift up her shield of faith against the giants secured by her Father's great love. The disciple's faith is her shield and protection against the fiery darts of doubt and fear. It is the only weapon that overcomes the giants that block her promised inheritance (1 John 5:4). This shield must be lifted even when it is heavy or when her arms are feeble and her muscles are weak.

When we encounter giants on our way to our promised inheritance we can choose, as Caleb chose, to see ourselves as defeated grasshoppers and head for the hills; or we can see ourselves as mighty warriors empowered by The God above all gods. The spies may have been conquered by fear but Joshua chose to serve the Lord and to obey in faith. Joshua trusted in the power of God Almighty as he moved out to claim his promised territory. He saw great victory as God was faithful to do all that he had promised. The kings of each of those warring tribes and many more were conquered and their lands were given as an inheritance to God's people (Joshua12,21:43-45). We can stand as Joshua stood and see the victory of the Lord.

Heart's Cry

Father, as I face great obstacles and giants help me to remember that you have allotted an inheritance to me. Remind me that as all the wealth of your kingdom and the power of your armies is mine when I present my needs at your throne. Help me to hold fast to your promises and to remember that you are faithful to do all that you say. Lord, give me persistent faith. Do not allow me to see myself as anything other than an overcomer because I belong to you and you have dominion over all things. Give me the faith and boldness needed to expect great things and to conquer the giants that you expose who are standing in my way. Amen.

Running the Race

Scripture Meditation

"Let us throw off everything that hinders and the sin that so easily entangles, and let us run with perseverance the race marked out for us."(Hebrews 12:1).

"Consider it pure joy, my brothers, whenever you face trials of many kinds, because you know that the testing of your faith develops perseverance."(James 1:2-3).

"I have fought a good fight, I have finished the race, and I have kept the faith."(2 Timothy 4:7).

Musing

A distance runner is an athlete who has learned to measure her speed. She will not surge up abruptly from her starting block in full strength only to tire out and to fail in her attempt to complete the entire course set before her. She calculates her pace and controls her breathing to keep both steady and constant. She studies her course and takes inventory of her skills. She assesses how, where and when she will push herself and when she will govern or pull back. Both her speed and her power must be controlled to assure that she will have the energy to go the distance and the stamina to reach her goal. She must also balance her body tension with her agility and flexibility. Strong legs, lungs and heart, flexible ankles and knees, and relaxed feet are all essential parts contributing to the overall success of her run. Her skill as she orchestrates the rise and fall of each forward step, the length of her stride and the weight of each step's impact is like that of a musical composer crafting a complex symphony or multi-part melody. She interacts with her environment in an athletic ballet as each aspect of her performance is studied, refined and uniquely fit together to form the completed dance. She recognizes that the dance must be performed one step at a time and that the course will be completed one step at a time. She knows the level of conditioning that each performance will require and she will stop her work only when she glides across that finish line with elegance and dignity.

To become a disciplined runner, one must enjoy the physical ardors of running. Such an athlete will find joy in the activity of conditioning; otherwise she will not continue to do the required training regardless of level of pain, and the sweat and the tiredness that she feels. At every turn, and at any moment, the race might present her with a difficulty and an unexpected challenge. If she is not prepared and her body and mind are left unconditioned such a challenge might cost her the victory and the accomplishment of her goal. So, she coaches herself with words of encouragement as she correctly nourishes her body, manages her time, disciplines her heart, mind and limbs, and schedules her life around the practice of running.

Running must become a joy of the heart and an experience that the disciplined runner has come to look forward to with anticipation and longing. She must desire the goal set before her enough to endure the stress running causes to her body. If she does not love the work of greater discipline and training, then each time that she misses a step, trips, or falls and skins her knees she will be tempted to give up and to never lace her shoes again. She runs *toward* the goal of her heart. It is not fear of failure that propels her forward nor is running a tedious feat. She runs for the *sheer joy* of running and for the goal set before her. The accomplished runner runs because she can and because she must. She is at the very core of her being- a runner.

And so it is with our journey from glory to glory as we are being transformed more completely into a closer reflection of our Lord (2 Corinthians 3:18). We cannot be haphazard in our discipline or grow weary in our training. We must lift our shield of faith though our arms are tired and our knees are weak (2 Samuel 22:35,Isaiah 35:3). We must stand our ground and distribute our weight as we dig in to stake our claim in our promised territory (Ephesians 6:13). We must ask the Lord to be our victory as He makes our faith and our strength match our assignment

(Psalm 27:1,1 Corinthians 15:57). Our course may lead us through rough terrain and over a rocky climb; but the Lord can and will equip us to scale with hinds feet and to leap with the heart of a gazelle (2 Samuel 22:34). God promises that He will steady our gait and establish our steps as He breathes newness of life into our tired bodies and languished spirits (2 Samuel 22:37). He will keep us from falling (Jude 1:24). He will strengthen our legs as the cedars of Lebanon as He guides us through this present time of trial and of testing into His glorious kingdom (Psalm 92:12, Acts 14:22). We will complete our course with great joy as we look into our Savior's face and focus upon His eyes. We will receive the treasure that He has for us as we complete our course in faith (2 Timothy 4:8). Hallelujah.

Heart's Cry

Father God, teach me to condition myself like an athlete as I nourish my spirit with your Word and discipline my will with your truth. I am no spiritual giant; you know that I am only spit and clay. Help me to know your strength and to believe that I can accomplish what you have set before me as I lift this clay pot up for you to fill. Give me joy for the race ahead as I place my hope in you. Help me to see you in the pathways that I take. Establish my steps. Be my companion on this journey. Transform me as you move me closer to the completion and fulfillment of my goals. Give me victory through the expansion of your life living within me. Amen

Fellowshipping within a Dysfunctional Flock

Scripture Meditation

"You shall love the Lord your God with all your heart, and with all your soul, and with your entire mind"; and, "You shall love your neighbor as yourself."(Matt. 22:37,29).

"As a prisoner for the Lord, then, I urge you to live a life worthy of the calling you have received. Be completely humble and gentle; be patient, bearing with one another in love. Make every effort to keep the unity of the Spirit through the bond of peace. There is one body and one Spirit, just as you were called to one hope when you were called; one Lord, one faith, one baptism; one God and Father of all, who is over all and through all and in all. But to each one of us grace has been given as Christ apportioned it. This is why it says: "When he ascended on high, he took many captives and gave gifts to his people." (What does "he ascended" mean except that he also descended to the lower, earthly regions? He who descended is the very one who ascended higher than all the heavens, in order to fill the whole universe.) So Christ himself gave the apostles, the prophets, the evangelists, the pastors and teachers, to equip his people for works of service, so that the body of Christ may be built up until we all reach unity in the faith and in the knowledge of the Son of God and become mature, attaining to the whole measure of the fullness of Christ."(Ephesians 4:1-13).

"Finally, all of you, be like-minded, be sympathetic, love one another, be compassionate and humble."(1 Peter 3:8).

"Whatever happens, conduct yourselves in a manner worthy of the gospel of Christ. Then, whether I come and see you or only hear about you in my absence, I will know that you stand firm in one spirit, contending as one man for the faith of the gospel ."(Philippians 1:27).

"Therefore if you have any encouragement from being united with Christ, if any comfort from his love, if any common sharing in the Spirit, if any tenderness and compassion, then make my joy complete by being like-minded, having the same love, being one in spirit and of one mind. Do nothing out of selfish ambition or vain conceit. Rather, in humility value others above yourselves, not looking to your own interests but each of you to the interests of the others."(Philippians 2:1-4).

Musing

I half-jokingly told the Lord the other day that I could do this walking in humility thing perfectly if he would not require that I do it with and around other people. The problem with my above admitted attitude is that there is no such thing as living out the Christian life as a lone ranger or as a solitary sojourner. Each child of God is required to be a contributing member of the Body of Christ. While many of us may believe that the choice to come to salvation is an individual decision, and that Jesus is our *personal* savior ; maturing as a disciple requires that we connect with a body of believers and begin utilizing our spiritual gifts and talents for the benefit and growth of all (1 Corinthians 12:7). A cursory read of Paul's letters to the early churches establishes that if we truly love the Lord, then we must recognize that we are united to one another as His body. According to God's plan, we were each saved into a family, grafted into a people group, and made joint heirs *together* with Christ Jesus (Romans 8:17, Romans 12:4-5, Hebrews chapters 5 through 8). Each of us is the member of a Royal Priesthood of believers (1 Peter 2:9). Like it or not; it is impossible to live our lives according to God's Word and to remain forever detached from the Lord's people and from His church. Detached body parts wither and die without the life giving blood flowing through them. Detached Christians follow that same pattern. We need the fellowship an encouragement of one another.

Let's face it; God's family *is* a dysfunctional one and the above call to godly unity just seems impossible when considering some of those who belong to the Body of Christ. His family is composed of insecure, down-trodden, broken, bruised, crippled, and all manner of otherwise damaged or disenfranchised sinners. Our interaction with one another is often marked by emotional outbursts, hurt feelings, shunning, gossip and avoidance as we fear rejection and disapproval and long to be recognized and praised for our hard work. I have often asked the Lord to explain how it can be that certain folks within the family of God are the source of so much frustration and irritation for me. Some of these "spiritual relatives" can get under my skin, evoke emotional outbursts in me, and irritate me to the point of sin. They are antagonistic, argumentative and stubborn. I fail to understand why it is that I must esteem them when they don't seem to esteem me. I suddenly find myself standing before God's throne complaining of His *unfair* request that I model His love to those who do not love me in return. I am twelve years old all over again and complaining about being forced to "play nicely" with my baby brother. I am indignant and bothered by the requirement that I extend my grace to someone so immature and undeserving.

It is at this point that the Holy Spirit gently reminds me that I am a member of the same family as these who irritate me and as such bear many of the same flawed character traits. As human beings, we can each thank our earthly father, Adam, for our on-going family feud and for the dysfunctional family members with whom we are now called to interact. Each one of us have a fallen heredity and an inherited sin nature through Adam that keeps us from operating as God intended for the members of His family (Genesis 3:6,Romans 3:23,Romans 5:12). Mankind's fall into disobedience has resulted in an eternal dysfunction in our relationship with God and with one another. We are all flawed and fallible, quirky, irrational, emotional, and dysfunctional. None of us is without sin, and we are all in need of the redemptive and restorative grace of Jesus Christ.

The hard truth is that if we are to obey the will of our Father then it will not be enough for us to simply tolerate some of the members of God's family while seeking to avoid others. We are instructed not to allow our fellowship to be dictated by our natural affinities (James 2:1-3). Following Christ will require that we show visible affection to everyone and that we honor each member of God's family more than we honor ourselves (Romans 12:10,16:16). It will be impossible for us to live and work within the church and totally avoid those people who irritate us or who try our patience and stretch our faith. Perhaps a better choice is to willingly decide to interact with those who appear irrational, impossible or otherwise dysfunctional. Doing so may actually serve a purpose in our spiritual growth by providing lessons that expose our own flaws, refine us and encourage our spiritual maturity (Proverbs 27:17). Likewise, establishing and following Biblical guidelines for settling disagreements or conflict between individuals and within the corporate Body, will provide opportunity for God's children to learn to pray for one another, to exercise grace in the presence of sin, and to seek God's gift of reconciliation and restoration (1 Corinthians 11:17-19). Scripture is very clear regarding our need to forgive the trespasses of others if we desire to be forgiven (Luke 11:4). Seeking God's wisdom and instruction in relationship difficulties ensures that God's children are not doomed to a life of hostile interactions and dysfunctional relationships. His love covers a multitude of sin (1 Peter 4:8).

The good news for the Body of Christ is that our dysfunctions are covered by the restorative act of Christ's sacrifice and the gift of His unmerited love toward us. Our inheritance shifts at the point of salvation from the inheritance of Adam to the inheritance of Christ's righteousness (1 John 1:7-8). We are forgiven and then rightly related to God and to others because of Christ's saving grace (John 3:16, 2 Corinthians 5:17-19). While it is true that we inherited our dysfunction(our sinful nature) because of the fall, it is equally true that in Christ Jesus we have the power to overcome these sinful behaviors and flawed personality traits (James 5:16, Romans 15:14). We are not doomed to our dysfunction or held captive by our sinful nature. We can choose not to give in to our sinful nature and can help our ugly attitudes towards others. The moment each of us received Jesus as our Savior, and acknowledged Him as Lord of our life, the Holy Spirit entered us and we were reconciled to God (Ephesians 1:13-14).The Holy Spirit then began the process of transforming us into a closer resemblance to that of our heavenly Father and away from our earthy father (2 Corinthians 3:18,5:17). It is because of this truth that members of the family of God must hold ourselves and each other accountable for our behavior. We must do so while exercising unmerited love toward one another. We don't get a free pass for our temper tantrums nor or we excused for failing to control our emotions or to exercise grace in our interactions. The transformative work of the Holy Spirit should result in a change in how we think as well as in how we interact with one another. We are now called to living lives that please our Father and that bring honor and glory to Him (Romans 12:1-2,Galatians 2:20).

The interactions between members of God's family are governed or constrained by the level of our willingness to walk with one another as Christ Jesus walked on the earth. He is our standard and our role-model. We are to imitate the attitude of service, grace and humility that Jesus Christ displayed in all His interactions (Mark 10:45,Ephesians 5:1-19). Despite what dysfunctions may exist within our heavenly family, as God's children we are instructed to engage in acts of kindness toward each other and to forgive one another to the same level in which Christ forgave us (Ephesians 4:32,Colossians 3:13). Christian brothers and sisters are called to exhibit God's love in *all* of our family interactions and to be mindful of the needs of those around us (1 Thessalonians 3:12). These are the outward signs of spiritual maturity, of living a life empowered by the Holy Spirit, and of being yielded to the will of God. Growing in Christ means putting away childish reactions and attitudes (1Corinthians 13:11).

As followers of Christ, we are called to accept a life of service and sacrifice to one another, even when it is not comfortable for us to do so, and even if we feel wronged or misunderstood(Galatians 6:2-6). The call to mature discipleship will require that our attitude and service be extended to those within the Body of Christ for whom we have no natural affinity and must include those for whom we may have outright distain as well as those whom we know do not naturally care for us (Matthew 5:43-48). This attitude of humility and grace will come more easily when we realize that we share the same inheritance of Adam as do those family members who irritate us. It could be that our own sinful pride, stubbornness and arrogance is the trigger that brings out the worst in those around us. Each of us must be willing to humbly accept our faults and to concede that we may be the difficult person in the lives of our brothers and sisters whom they are discussing with the Lord. We must seek to display unity of mind and humility in our attitude while we ask the Lord to expose sin; in us as well as in others, and to repair and restore damaged relationships (Philippians 2:2).

As we mature in the faith we must realize that greater responsibility is placed upon those of us who have positions of leadership teaching and discipling others (Luke 17:2, Colossians 1:28-29). We want to be careful not to become critical of our younger family members and to cause discouragement by binding them to legalisms, dogma, and disputable doctrines (Romans 14:1-22). Likewise, more mature Christians need to live in a manner that does not cause younger brothers and sisters to falter or sin. Scripture indicates that God places greater responsibility on those who are mature for maintaining unity within the Body of Christ. We want to make every effort to imitate Christ in our walk, as well as to teach and to establish those who are younger in the faith (Colossians 3:16). We need to exercise the fruit of the spirit and to exhibit the grace of God as we lovingly train up God's children (Galatians 5:22-26, Ephesians 4:1-7). Then and only then will it be possible for us to fulfill the will of God and to love others as our Father first loved us (1 John 4:19).

Heart's Cry

Father, in humility teach me to seek the things of Christ rather than to fulfill my own selfish and prideful desires. Help me to put away childish and petty emotions and thinking and to grow up into all that you desire of me. Help me by the power of the Holy Spirit to crucify self-love and self-orientation and to be mindful of the needs and hurts of those around me. Give me a servant's heart and a humble attitude. I lay my will and my rights at your feet. Empty me of self and make me a vessel of blessing and of service to you. Amen

Samuel's Victory Song

You are my lamp o Lord: the Lord turns my darkness into light.

With your help I can advance against a troop, with my God I can scale a wall.

As for the Lord, His way is perfect; the word of the Lord is flawless.

He is a shield for all who take refuge in Him.

For who is God besides the Lord? And who is the Rock except our God?

It is God who arms me with strength and makes my way perfect.

He makes my feet like the feet of a deer; he enables me to stand on the heights.

He trains my hands for battle; my arms can bend a bow of bronze.

You give me your shield of victory; you stoop down to make me great.

You broaden the path beneath me; so that my ankles do not turn-

2 Samuel 22:29-27

Closing Thoughts
From the Disciple

"My lover spoke and said to me, "Arise, my darling, my beautiful one, and come with me." (Song of Solomon 2:10).

Each disciple daughter's journey here on earth is lived out through a series of transitions and changes. Those transitions will occur within our relationships and in our sense of connectedness to others. As we move through our lives there will be seasons of rich friendships intermingled with periods of isolation. As we grow up into all that God has created in us sooner or later He will call us to come away with Him into a period designed to be a time of preparation, refining, and of deeper revelation. Every disciple daughter can anticipate at least one such *calling away* or time of separation in her lifetime.

These calls to go away with God should not be dreaded and viewed as entrance into periods of dryness or of desert. They should not be viewed as punishment or harsh treatment but rather as opportunities to grow and to learn new things about ourselves and about our creator. Being alone with God is never intended to be lonely and shouldn't be if we are counting Him as all sufficient.

Because God loves every disciple daughter, He will initiate times in our lives that can serve to draw us closer to Him and to deepen our intimacy with Him. The periods of isolation and separation that we experience in our life journey have an express purpose in God's ultimate plan for us. Our Father draws us close to Himself to increase our courage, strengthen our faith, deepen our wisdom and discernment, and broaden our knowledge of Him. God also uses these times away to smooth out all the remaining rough edges of our personality or attitude, to refine our behavior, and to demolish any trace of an idol or stronghold of the enemy. The beloved daughter of God should seek to embrace these times, no matter how difficult, as divine appointments and thank her Father for these blessed opportunities for spiritual growth and development. These times of stretching and refinement can provide the disciple with a deeper walk with the Father because by walking through them she will come to see her God as all sufficient, ever present and ever faithful.

Every sojourner knows that setting out on a journey requires the willing act of moving from one's present location in a chosen direction. Going on a journey implies going away, making a transition or traveling forward. The first step in moving forward always requires that the traveler be willing to leave the old behind and to venture toward what lies ahead. The attitude of a disciple who desires to journey forward with the Lord must be one that embraces newness and welcomes change because God always desires to do a new thing in the life and soul of His willing child. The willingness to accept change and to be transformed by the Father is the beginning step of the long trek across the Desert of Transition into the fullness of all that God has for His disciple daughter.

Learning to trust while traveling through rough terrain and to patiently wait for God to reveal His plan while enveloped in muddled fogs of confusion can be quite difficult, but we can be encouraged if we remember that faith is a walk and growth is a process. There will be stops and starts intermingled with slow movement and quick accomplishments. Some legs of our journey will be more difficult that others and some tasks will require more faith and surrender than others. The Christian life is one of forever being changed and of growing up as our heavenly Father transforms us from glory to glory into a closer reflection of Him. All of this is accomplished in His sovereign timing and as He wills. Transformation is an ongoing process that does not end until we see His face.

It is inevitable that each disciple will each go through times of testing and stretching as we follow Christ. Faith is a muscle that must be exercised and patience is developed through perseverance. When we feel pushed and pulled, pressed down or stretched to the point of breaking we should consider such periods in our lives as the assurance that God has not taken His hand from us. We are still the clay being molded in the potter's hands. Our Father is still busily at work in the process of refining us for His future service. He is transforming us into a glorious vessel to serve an express purpose that He has in mind. We can relax, relinquish control to His strong hands, and yield to the pressure of our creator's touch. It is not His desire to crush us or to destroy us. It is His will to transform us into something beautiful that brings Him glory.

Remember, it has always been part of God's routine to walk together with His creation. From the very beginning, God would come to the Garden of Eden to walk in the evening dew with His first beloved man, Adam (Genesis 3:8). Recall how God was deeply saddened when Adam and Eve hid themselves away and ran from His presence after they had disobeyed His will for them and succumbed to the temptations of sin. Their creator desired fellowship and intimacy with His creation even as they hid in the thicket and sought to hide their nakedness. He is still saddened today when His daughters hide away or fear His call to come to Him. We run from His desire for time spent in intimate fellowship because we dread the rigors of His demands rather than anticipate the joy of spending time in His presence.

Dear Disciple Daughter, even as your traveling takes you through the widest expanse of wilderness and across the most arid of all deserts, remember that sometimes digging deeply enough into the hot, dry, desert sand will reveal an underground artesian stream of living water. Often upon closer examination even the most desolate and lonely environments can be found to be teeming with life. If we can discipline ourselves to use these times of separation to dig more deeply into the truth of God's Word and to drink fully from the Holy Spirit's assurance we will find that we are anchored in God's promises and sustained by His character. We will also discover that our intended desert environment has opened up as an oasis of refreshment and renewal in the Lord's presence. May we then reflect upon our Father's goodness as we gather up the precious memory stones that lined our journey's path and build an altar of praise to The Lord's excellent name (Exodus 24:4-18,Hebrews 9:15-20). Our God has been faithful.

Royal Heritage

I am the Daughter of Jehovah-Shalom
He is the God of the mountain and the sea.
I speak,
and He stretches forth His strong hand to make it so.
And I cry out to Him that He might destroy my enemies.

I am the grafted vine into the Hebrew nation.
The life-blood of royalty flow through my veins.
I am rightly clothed in purple and perfumed with myrrh.
Those who scoffed at me must now bow their heads as they behold my royal lineage.

My Father commends His armies to me.
Ten thousand warriors walk by my side.
I speak the Word and they draw swords to avenge me.
None can rise up against the majesty and skill of my Father's legions.
They are fierce men of battle, skilled and greatly armored.
They ride on steads with swift feet and proud necks.

My protector soars above with wings of eagles.
He flies high to shadow me in His mighty wingspread
from the heat of the noon day sun.
In the evening He warms me neath the downy feathers of His breast.
When my destroyer seeks me, he finds me not.
For I am hidden neath the folds of my Father's wings.

Surely as I walk the numbered days of my life,
I shall walk the steps of His ordained path.
And when these temporal days are ended…
Then with trumpet call shall He lift me and carry me
home to live forever at His side.

For I am the Daughter of Jehovah- Shalom.
He is the One True God.

About the Author

Cinthia W. Pratt, M.A. Leadership in Higher Education, Sociology

Cindee left a successful and award winning faculty position within a university Sociology department after feeling called by the Lord to take her knowledge and skillset out of the secular classroom and into the heart of God's women. She says that it is her heart's desire to help God's women discover who they are in Christ Jesus and to then develop and maintain healthy intimate relationships with their creator and with others. Cindee finds it sad that most women cannot declare with full assurance that they are "*fearfully and wonderfully made*" (Psalm 139:14).

Cindee believes that we can't love others until we first recognize the great love of God for us and then learn to love ourselves as His designer creation. The focus of her ministry is to offer a knowledgeable, reassuring and honest voice of encouragement and empowerment to women of all ages and at various phases of life. Her teaching uses humor and illustrations drawn from the female perspective to provide helpful tools and life-changing truths to help women to become all that God created them to be. She longs to work alongside pastors, lay-leaders, community organizations and churches to replace the half-truths and misconceptions about what it means to be a woman that are being circulated within our popular culture today.

Cindee would love to come and share with the Fearfully Wonderful women of your church or community group. You will find additional information regarding Cindee's speaking and teaching ministry as well as about obtaining copies of the other books that she has authored by visiting her website at: becomingallgodcreated.org. You might also want to join in the conversations with the members of the *encouragement entourage* who gather there.

If you would like additional information or to speak with Cindee directly about planning the perfect workshop, conference or seminar for your group please contact her at fearfullyfemale@gmail.com.

NOTES

All of the artwork contained in this book are the original oil paintings of Cindee and are offered up in worship to the Lord.

CPSIA information can be obtained at www.ICGtesting.com
Printed in the USA
BVOW071837110912

300158BV00003B/4/P